Al-Islam

Christianity

&

Freemasonry

by Mustafa El-Amin

Published by:

New Mind Productions
P. O. Box 5185
Jersey City, NJ 07305

Copyright © By Mustafa El-Amin

ISBN 0-933821-05-0

First Edition — December, 1985
Second Printing — February, 1986
Third Printing — July, 1987
Fourth Printing — August 1988
Fifth Printing — May 1990
Sixth Printing--August 1990

DEDICATION

This work is dedicated to those fearless men and women who stand up for truth, patience, and human dignity. It is also dedicated to the opressed masses who yearn for total freedom and responsibility. Most importantly, this work is dedicated to the sincere Muslims and Believers who are working tiredlessly to establish a sound Islamic community here in America, based on the Holy Qur'an and the Sunnah (Way) of Prophet Muhammad (PBUH).

Many efforts and achievements are being made to present a clear message of Al-Islam to the American people and the world. It is our hope that this work will be a contributing factor in such noble efforts.

There are many people who have been helpful to the development and completion of this book, however space will only allow me to mention a few.

I would like to first thank my wife Joanne S. El-Amin, for all of her encouragement, support, and patience. I would like to also thank Brothers Ansari Nadir, Omar Bey Ali, Hakim Ali, Khalif Abdur-Rashed, and Hakeem Bilal for their profound advice and prudent recommendations in the area of research and religious thought.

Last, but not least, I would like to extend my most sincerest appreciation and gratitude to Brother Imam Muhammad Armiya Nu'Man and his wife Zakiyyah Nu'Man for typesetting, editing, and advancing this project, and many other worthy books to their completion.

FOREWORD

This book, AL-ISLAM, CHRISTIANITY, & FREEMASON-
RY, by Mustafa El-Amin is a book that I am sure will create
quite a controversy among those who would not like to see
it published. It contains much of the secrets of a organization
that has had more influence on the modern world, than perhaps, many of the bonified religions.

The author does an in depth study on the religions of
Al-Islam and Christianity, and shows how the people who
practice Freemasonry "borrowed" from the religions to set
up their own "playground". His critique of the evolution
of Al-Islam, from the time of Prophet Muhammad (Peace
Be Upon Him), in Arabia, to today's modern leader, Imam
Warith Deen Muhammad, in America, shows how its growth
has been natural and necessary for the advance of the real
life of the human being.

In his examination of the religion of Christianity, the
author demonstrates how "Modern" Christianity came to
be with the Emperor Constantine, and the Nicene Council.
This is an eye-opener for those who have little or no knowledge
about the mechanics that produced this way of life for millions
of people. Written out of respect, and not condemnation,
he shows how people have tampered with the very fabric
of most people's beliefs just to meet selfish gains.

On the other hand, his showing how a group of people
taking just the portions of the religion that could fit their
purposes, and leaving the rest, just using religious "trappings",
have put together one of the most powerful movements
on earth, Freemasonry. This movement of Freemasonry,
involved some of the best minds that the Western World
has produced, and yet, they did not necessarily use their
knowledge for the advancement of human society, but to
keep the masses of the world in ignorance and darkness.
This is to be abhorred. Especially for a Mason or Shriner

to say, "If children can play Cowboys and Indians, we can play Muslims and Infidels", is a gross misuse of something that is held sacred by so many people.

This exposé on Freemasonry has been long overdue, and I hope the reader will understand it for what it is really worth.

Imam Muhammad Armiya Nu'Man
November, 1985

TABLE OF CONTENTS

AL-ISLAM

AL-ISLAM, CHRISTIANITY, AND FREEMASONRY

THE RELIGION OF AL-ISLAM

"So set thy face steadily and truly to the Faith: (Establish) God's handiwork according to the pattern on which He has made mankind: No change (let there be) in the work (wrought) by God: that is the standard religion: but most among mankind understand not." Holy Qur'an 30:30

Al-Islam is the natural way of life for all of humanity. It is the religion or pattern on which Allah (God) established creation. The word, **"Islam"**, actually means "peace and submission". Everything in creation submits to the Will of the Creator. The sun, the moon, the stars, the birds, and the bees all submit to the command of Allah. The Holy Qur'an says, **"To Him belongs every being that is in the heavens and on earth: All are devoutly obedient to Him"**. (1) It also tells us in Surah (Chapter) 26, Verses 41 and 42, that all the creation gives praise to Allah. It reads, **"Seest thou not that it is God whose praise all beings in the heavens and on earth do celebrate, and the birds (of the air) with wings outspread? Each one knows its own (mode of) prayer and praise. And God knows well all that they do. ...Yea, to God belongs the dominion of the heavens and the earth; and to God is the final goal (of all)."** (2) That which submits to the Creator is called "Muslim". Therefore, the Moon, the Sun, the Stars and all of creation can actually be called Muslim because it has that Muslim or submissive nature inherent in its essences.

Every human being is born a Muslim. It is reported that Prophet Muhammad said that we are all born Muslims, but it is our environment that makes us other than that. Although we are all Muslims in our biological human nature,

-1-

we cannot realize our true and complete Muslim nature until we consciously and willingly conform to what the Creator has willed. It is only then that we become Muslims in our heart and in our mind.

Al-Islam is designed to appeal to our intellect so that we will be able to make the best use of our lives. In his book, **Prayer and Al-Islam**, Imam W. Deen Muhammad points out that Al-Islam is not just a religion of faith, he states, "It is a rational religion of knowledge and logic. It is the fulfillment of the mission of all the prophets who led society to a faith that recognizes the existence of the One Creator, and the obligation of every creature to him." (3)

All of the Prophets of God were Muslims. They all bowed their wills to the Will of the Creator. They all taught the Oneness of Allah. Allah says in the Qur'an, **"And this was the legacy that Abraham left to his sons, and so did Jacob; Oh my sons, God hath chosen the faith for you, then die not except in the Faith of Al-Islam."** (4)

Allah also tells us in the Holy Qur'an that not only were all the Prophets and Messengers Muslim, but they all belong to one brotherhood, and that we should not make any difference between them. **"We gave Moses the Book and followed clear (signs) and strengthened him with the Holy Spirit. O, Ye Apostles! enjoy (all) things good and pure, and work righteousness: For I am well acquainted with (all) that ye do, and verily this Brotherhood of yours is a single Brotherhood, and I am your Lord and Cherisher: Therefore fear Me (and no other)."** (5)

In Surah 3, Ayat 84, it reads, **"Say: 'We believe in Allah and in what was revealed to Abraham, Ismail; Isaac, Jacob, and the Tribes, and in (the Books) given to Moses, Jesus, and the Prophets, from their Lord: We make no distinction between one and another among them, and to Allah do we bow our will (in Islam)."**

Those of us who consciously profess and declare ourselves Muslims and believers have an obligation to shine the light of our religion throughout the world. We have to meet the challenge. We must let this world know the true ideas, concepts, beliefs and achievements of Al-Islam. Prophet Muhammad said that a Muslim desires for his fellow brethren that which he desires for himself.

Imam W. Deen Muhammad said in a lecture on January 18, 1981 that "Al-Islam is a door of Freedom" (and freedom can be understood to mean Free-dom, the freedom to develop the mind with truth and knowledge). Hammudah Abdalati points out in his book **Islam In Focus** that the true Muslim believes that man must work out his salvation through the guidance of God. "This means that in order to attain salvation, a person must combine Faith and action, belief and practice."(6) It is reported that Prophet Muhammad said it is better to teach knowledge one hour of the day than it is to pray all night long. The Holy Qur'an says, concerning the propagation of truth and righteousness, "Let there arise out of you a band of people inviting to all that is good, enjoining what is right, and forbidding what is wrong: They are the ones to attain felicity." (3:104) Allah says: "Invite (all) to the Way of thy Lord with wisdom and beautiful preaching." (16:125)

Man's Struggle For Truth and Understanding

Ever since man has been on this planet, he has had to battle the forces of ignorance and injustice. In his natural development he has to battle his environment. History tells us that prehistoric man feared the forces of nature. He feared the lightning, the thunder, rain, hail, and snow. He also feared the gigantic animals and reptiles. This environmental fear, however, was not due to injustice, but to ignorance. The environment serves as a challenge to the human being to grow and develop as the vicegerent and khalifah on earth. The natural environment also serves as a body of knowledge, with its many signs for man to learn from. It is through our interaction with the physical environment that our mind and intellect grows and develops. Imam W. Deen Muhammad explained sometime ago, in an article

-3-

entitled <u>Knowledge of Creation</u>, that, "In order to know your place in the glorious creation of Almighty God's creation, we must know the truth of creation. The knowledge of creation enables you to master creation." (7)

The Holy Qur'an, The Clear Evidence, says, **"Behold, in the creation of the heavens and the earth, and in the alternation of night and day, there are indeed signs for men of understanding..."** (3:190)

The human being, as a physical creature, depends greatly upon his senses for his development in this physical world. As human beings, we receive messages from the creation through our five senses: (sight, hearing, feelings, smell, and taste).

Dr. Na'im Akbar, explains in his book, **The Community of Self,** that "Almost at the time of birth, the person begins to establish contact with the outer world by way of the body's windows known as the senses...sight, hearing, smell, taste, and touch, the channels through which the self receives messages from the outer world. Without these windows into the world, the community of self would be locked behind a wall of darkness, silence, and complete isolation from the beautiful and informative physical world which surrounds us." (p.4)

Imam Armiya Nu'Man of Jersey City, in keeping with the spirit of the Qur'an and the Sunnah of Prophet Muhammad (PBUH), in one of his Islamic Studies classes, expounded upon the ways in which the human being receives knowledge. He pointed out that one of the ways is through our five senses, observation of creation. Other ways Imam Nu'Man pointed out were through revelation, inspiration, and authority, i.e. parents, teachers, etc.

Aside from the natural challenges and hardships that the creation tests man with, jealousy, pride, and arrogance also serve as a challenge to the human being. The Bible tells us that God created man and woman and placed them

-4-

in the garden, and commanded them saying, "of every tree of the garden thou mayest freely eat; But of the tree of the **knowledge of good and evil**, thou shalt not eat of it; for in the day that thou eatest thereof, thou shalt surely die." The Serpent, who was more clever than all the other creatures, began to plot and plan to bring the man and society down from its dignified place in the world. "**Now the serpent was more subtle than any beast of the field which God had made...and the serpent said unto the woman, "Ye shall not surely die. For God doth know that in the day ye eat thereof, then your eyes shall be opened, and ye shall be as gods knowing good and evil.**" (Gen. 3, Verses 1-6)

Here, we see a deliberate attempt to deceive and destroy man and society, as well as, an open rebellion against the Word of God.

The Holy Qur'an explains it this way:

"**Behold, thy Lord said to the angels: 'I will create a vicegerent in the earth'. They said, 'Wilt thou place therein one who will make mischief therein and shed blood? Whilst we do celebrate Thy praises and glorify Thy Holy (name)?' He said, 'I know what you know not!'**"

The next verse says, "**And He taught Adam the nature of all things; then He placed them before the angels and said: 'Tell me the nature of these if ye are right.' They said, 'Glory to Thee: of knowledge we have none, save what Thou hast taught us: in truth it is Thou who art perfect in knowledge and wisdom.' He said, 'O Adam! Tell them their natures.' When Adam had told them, God said: 'Did I not tell you that I know the secrets of the heavens and the earth, and I know what ye reveal and what ye conceal?'**"

"**And Behold, We said to the angels, 'Bow down to Adam': and they bowed down: Not so Iblis: he refused and was haughty: He was of those who reject Faith.**" (2:30-34)

"**God said, 'O Iblis! What is your reason for not being among those who prostrated themselves?' (Iblis) said: 'I am** not one to prostrate myself to man, whom Thou did create from sounding clay, from mud moulded into shape.' God said: 'Then get thee out from here: for thou are rejected, accursed. And the curse shall be on thee till the Day of Judgement.' (Iblis) said: 'O my Lord! Give me then respite till the day the (dead) are raised.' God said: 'Respite is granted thee—till the Day of the Time Appointed.' (Iblis) said: 'O my Lord! Because Thou hast put me in the wrong, I will make (wrong) fair-seeming to them on the earth, and I will put them all in the wrong.—Except Thy servants among them sincere and purified (By Thy Grace).'" (2:32-40).

Man is created, according to the word of God, in the best of moulds. Man is not born sinful. The concept of "Original Sin" is rejected in Al-Islam. The Holy Qur'an teaches that man can grow and develop to a high plane of dignity as long as he accepts, respects and follows the guidance of God. However, if we reject the guidance of God we can fall to the lowest of the low. Both the Bible and the Qur'an show us that when the Creator created the human being, Satan (a diabolical and rebellious mind) immediately declared war on the human being. The struggle in the world has been/is between Truth and Falsehood. It is a struggle between those who want to oppress and enslave the human mind and those who want to enlighten and free the human mind, to dignify the human being as Allah has intended. Allah says in Al-Qur'an "They plan a plan, and Allah plans a plan, and Allah is the best of planners."

The prophets and messengers of God were the forerunners in the battle for human freedom and growth. They were like valiant roosters, the first to awaken with the light of truth, calling the rest of humanity to awaken to the dictates of God.

The prophets of God were men of good character and high honor. They were prepared by the Creator to deliver His message to mankind. Their aim was to serve God, to acquaint man with God and His Divine plan; to establish truth and righteousness; to help man come to realize the true purpose of his existence, and help him to conduct his life in the purposeful manner in which God wants him to. Although many of the prophets came at different times and to different groups of people, they all taught one message of Truth, the Oneness of God. Imam W.D. Muhammad has explained on several occasions that the succession of prophethood actually represents the various stages of development in the human being and society. In a lecture entitled Truth That Lights The World, concerning the ascension of Prophet Muhammad wherein he met several prophets, beginning with Adam, the Imam explained:

"Here were men, at different stations of the heaven; and here is a prophet being taken to every station, then lastly, after visiting all the stations...a call was made that the prophets should come to prayer, and all the prophets from the different stations gathered together in prayer, and Prophet Muhammad went ahead of them and led them in prayer. Each one of them represent a natural development in human original nature, a development that God had himself inscribed into our growth pattern. But Prophet Muhammad was himself a unique person in the Prophethood. What is his unique place? He does not represent a step in human development, he represents what Jesus is a sign of--reconciliation. Once God has ordered human growth as it should be ordered, and the Tempter has broken that order and separated what God has made together--putting some of us in a spiritual bag and others in a material bag; some in a rational bag, some in a gnostic bag--- then Prophet Muhammad was sent to bring the clear light of understanding back so that the heavens could be ordered and reconciled with the earth once more. So God said to the heavens and the earth, "Come ye together." Through Prophet Muhammad they are brought together--balance, agreement, reconciliation. He is the Prophet of revelation; the others are the Prophets of development. Let us understand that. All the other Prophets lead up to Prophet Muhammad; development leads up to revelation. Once the society is developed properly, then the revelation is manifested, but first the natural chain of development must be completed."

Abraham: The Leader of The Nations

"And who turns away from the religion of Abraham but such as debase their souls with folly? Him we chose and rendered pure in the Hereafter in the ranks of the Righteous." (Holy Quran: Surah 2, Ayat 130).

"Behold my convenant is with thee, and thou shalt be a father of many nations. Neither shall thy name any more be called Abram, but thy name shall be Abraham; for a father of many nations have I made thee." (Bible: Chapter 17, Verse 5).

Prophet Abraham/Ibrahim is considered to be the "Father of the Faithful" by Muslims, Christians and Jews. Abraham is declared as an ideal model for mankind. The order of religion of Prophet Muhammad is in line with the order of Prophet Abraham. The mission of Abraham was to preach the message of unity and the Oneness of Allah. According to Muhammad Shamim Raza, M.A., D.J., "The name of Ibrahim-Hebrew Abraham, meaning 'father of the multitude', "high father"--finds repeated mention (forty times) in the Holy Qur'an. He is declared as an ideal model for mankind. Ibrahim laid the foundation of the three great religions of the world, namely, Judaism, Christianity and Islam...His contribution to the cause of peace and prosperity can never be forgotten. He is ever green in the hearts of millions." (8)

As stated earlier, all of the prophets were muslims and practiced the religion of Al-Islam, however, the history of the life of Abraham gives us a clearer picture of the development of the religion of Al-Islam. According to history, Abraham was the son of Azar, whose occupation was carpentry and the making of and selling of statues for worship. Abraham was born in Mesopotamia (now called Iraq). The name Mesopotamia, some researchers say, means "the land between the rivers". The rivers are the Euphrates and Tigris.

Abraham Rejects Idol Worship

As young Abraham grew up and observed his father making idols for worship, he became dissatisfied with his people's worship and consecration of them. As his heart and conscience began to trouble him more because of this false worship, one day he went to his father and asked him to explain how he could worship that which his hands had fashioned. According to the history, Abraham was not satisfied with the answer that his father gave him. The more Abraham began to reflect on the conditions of his people, the more determined he became to change their conditions and their false idea of the Creator. "Accordingly, he sought to convince his people of the futility of idol worship with arguments and proof." Muhammad Husayn Haykal points out that, "Once he (Abraham) seized the opportunity of the absence of worshippers from the temple and destroyed all the statues of the gods except that of the principal deity." (9) When he was questioned in public about this crime, he invited them to use their intellect and sense of reasoning. He told them to ask the idol gods, for surely if they were indeed God, they would tell the worshippers who broke them to pieces. The Holy Qur'an puts it this way: "They said, "Art thou the one that did this with our gods, O Abraham?" He said: "Nay, this was done by—this is their biggest one! Ask them, if they can speak intelligently!" Then were they confounded with shame: (they said), "Thou knowest full well that these (idols) do not speak!" (Abraham) said, "Do ye then worship, beside Allah, things that can neither be of any good to you nor do you harm? Fie upon you, and upon the things that ye worship besides God! Have ye no sense?!" (H.Q. 21:62-67).

-9-

According to the history, Abraham's destruction of the idols came after he had given serious and constant reflection on the irrationality of idol worship and polytheism, and searched sincerely and diligently for the proper idea and object of worship.

According to Imam W.D. Muhammad, "A prophet is one who understands something of truth. He knows that there is a God and he feels the reality of a righteous being in his own life."(10) He also explains that, "God has always awakened the minds of good people to truth. When He awakens their minds, they carry that truth to people who are in mental darkness." (11)

Abraham: Guided to Proper Worship

Abraham, after trying diligently to persuade his father and his people to turn from idol worship, left his father's house and traveled to Palestine, and then to Egypt. However, before his migration, Allah blessed Abraham with the true concept of God and worship. Allah revealed to Prophet Muhammad in the Holy Qur'an concerning Abraham the following, "**So also did we show Abraham the power and the laws of the heavens and the earth, that he might (with understanding) have certitude**". (H. Q. 6:75)

Abraham began to come into the knowledge of the true God during the night. The Holy Qur'an explains the story as such, "**When the night covered him over he saw a star: He said: "This is my Lord". But when it set, He said: "I love not those that set." When he saw the moon rising in splendour, he said: "This is my Lord". But when the moon set, he said: "Unless my Lord guide me, I shall surely be among those who go astray." When he saw the sun rising in splendour, he said: "This is my Lord; This is the greatest (of all)." But when the sun set, He said, "O my people! I am indeed free from your (guilt) of giving partners to God." For me, I have set my face, firmly and truly towards Him who created the heavens and the earth, and never shall I give partners to God.**" (H.Q. 6:76-79)

Abraham was a man of unshakable faith. He was also a rational man who did not hesitate to disregard the worship of objects that were not worthy of worship. Imam W.D. Muhammad says, "Because Abraham had the original faith of Adam, that faith endured the test of logic. Logic's revelation was not too shaking to shake the faith."(12) Abraham represents the rational Muslim. We can see in Abraham the dawning of the rational conscience in man. As history tells us, he looked at the stars, the moon and the sun, and concluded that neither was God.

There is another important event that took place in the life of Abraham which shows his unquenchable desire for knowledge and understanding. According to the Holy Qur'an, Abraham cried out to the All Powerful Creator, **"My Lord! Show me how Thou givest life to the dead." Allah said: "Dost thou not then believe?"** And Abraham in a very humble and submissive manner responded: **"Yes! but to satisfy my own understanding."** Then the Creator instructed him to, **"take four birds and train them to 'turn to thee.' And then place a portion of them "on every hill and call them: They will come to thee (flying) with speed. Then know that Allah is exalted in Power, Wise".**

Muslims should demonstrate the same kind of willingness to learn and achieve knowledge and understanding, as Abraham did. Prophet Muhammad (Peace and Blessing of Allah forever be upon him) said, **"Knowledge is the lost property of the believer."** He also said, **"We should seek knowledge from the cradle to the grave."** We should never allow ourselves to become unenthused about pursuing knowledge and truth. Our religion tells us that we have an obligation to spread the message of Al-Islam. How can we teach the message of the Qur'an, the Sunnah of Prophet Muhammad, and the profound wisdom that is prevalent in the Creation, if we do not study and learn. It is reported that Prophet Muhammad (PBUH) said, **"Seek knowledge, even unto China".** We should ask Allah to bless us with faith (Iman) and understanding. Knowledge enables us to break the chains of ignorance and superstition.

The Creator invites us to ask questions and to seek answers, but He also cautions us not to become like the people of Moses, who questioned every move Moses made (See Holy Qur'an, Sura 2, Ayat 67-71). Solomon said, "Get knowledge and wisdom, but above all get understanding." Understanding allows us to know what stands under the knowledge, what supports the knowledge. Allah is the source of all knowledge.

Abraham's Sacrifice

Abraham was not only a man of logic and reason, he was also a man of faith. He was so sincere and dedicated to the Creator, that he was willing to sacrifice his only son, Isma'il, for the pleasure of Allah (God). According to the story of this great event, Abraham received a vision from Allah, the Lord of all the worlds, to sacrifice his son. Both he and his son, Isma'il, courageously agreed to carry out Allah's command. The Holy Qur'an says, "And when (his son) was old enough to walk with him, Abraham said, "O my dear son, I have seen in a dream that I must sacrifice you (The dreams of the Prophets convey the Orders of Allah), so look, what do you think?" He (Isma'il) said, "O my father! do that which you are commanded. Allah willing, you shall find me of the steadfast." (Holy Qur'an 37:102).

According to some reports, Satan approached Abraham and told him that what he saw in his vision was only a Satanic illusion that he may kill his son and grieve thereat the rest of his days. Abraham, however, dismissed him and cursed him. It has also been reported that Isma'il told his father, "Sit upon my shoulders so I do not harm you when the sharp blade strikes me, and turn my face towards the ground, and do not slay me while looking at my face least you should have a mercy for me." Still others report that Abraham tried to cut the back of his son's neck, but was unable to because the knife slipped several times. The Holy Qur'an says, "So when they had both submitted their wills (to God) and he had laid him prostrate on his forehead (for sacrifice), we called out to him, "O Abraham! Thou hast already fulfilled

-12-

the vision!" **Thus indeed do we reward those who do right."**
(13) Allah commanded Abraham to sacrifice a sheep instead
of Isma'il.

This story clearly shows Abraham's submissiveness to
the will and commands of Allah. "For this was obviously
a trial." The sacrificing of the sheep or ram, is not to be
misunderstood in any way, as a means of reaching the Most
High, Creator of the heavens and the earth. (See Holy Qur'an
22:37). Allah is reached by sincerity and honesty. The animal
is only a symbol of something within us, but is not wasted
when it dies. It is used to feed the poor. In Chapter 22,
"Hajj" of the Holy Qur'an, Allah tells us through Prophet
Muhammad (PBUH) that the meat of the slaughtered animal
is to be shared with the poor. Imam W. Deen Muhammad
says, "Allah was testing Abraham's willingness to sacrifice
his son in order to serve His divine order. When Allah stopped
Abraham from killing his son, He ordered him to sacrifice
the ram and feed it to the poor. This ram represents
Abraham's stability and sense of security in knowledge and
wealth. Through an open to all sacrifice, he raised the living
conditions of other people. Allah does not want us to kill
our children, but He does ask that our faith and love be
greater for Him than for our children. We should be willing
to sacrifice our desires, aspirations, inclinations and appetities
for His cause. We should willingly relegate all of our sentiments to Him." (14)

Concerning the sacrifice that Muslims make during
Hajj (Pilgrimage), which is taken after the sacrifice of Abraham, Imam W. Deen Muhammad explains, "This sacrifice
symbolically indicates that we, as individuals, are first responsible for ourselves. The shedding of blood symbolizes our
victory over the life drive of the animal nature within us.
We are not to be controlled by our animal instincts, desires
and appetites. We should rise to a high level. We should
discipline the life drives of our animal inclinations to yield
obedience to Allah."

Abraham was an obedient and faithful servant of Allah.
He rejected the false worship of his father and his people.

He was persecuted for his persistent and unshakable faith. He disregarded and rejected his original idea of God, when he received greater understanding and inspiration from the Creator of all things, the All Wise, Allah. He demonstrated, unequivocally, a sincere willingness to sacrifice his only son Isma'il, for the sake of Allah (God).

"Say: God speaketh the Truth: follow the religion of Abraham, the sane in faith; he was not of the pagans" -- Holy Qur'an

What Was the Sacrifice

Many researchers and writers give much time to the question of which one of Abraham's sons was sacrificed. The Christians believe it was Isaac, and many Muslims believe it was Isma'il. I am of the opinion and belief that it was Isma'il. Although the Bible states clearly that it was Isaac, it also says that Abraham was told to sacrifice his only son. Based on the Bible, at no time was Isaac Abraham's only son. Isma'il was his only son, he was born of an Egyptian woman named Hagar. Isaac was born later by Sarah who for a long time could not give birth. (See Bible Gen.16:15 and 21:5). According to the Bible, Abraham was eighty-six years old when he had Isma'il, and one hundred when Isaac was born. A difference of fourteen years. Based on this information presented in the Bible, anyone who claims to accept the Bible as the word of God, must agree that (1) Ismail was Abraham's only son at one time, thus the one to be sacrificed, or (2) that the Bible is filled with contradictions and is therefore not fit to be called the "Word of God."

More importantly than the issue of which son was to be sacrificed, is the idea or message that is to be learned from the story of Abraham. As already explained, this story shows us how sincere Abraham was and how sincere and faithful we who call ourselves Muslims and Believers should be. There is a very important principle promulgated in the idea of Sacrifice. To sacrifice is to give of something that belongs to you and is of some value to you. Knowledge is a valuable jewel. Allah says in the Qur'an, "Are the blind equal with those who see? Or the depths of darkness equal with light?" (Qur'an 13:16). The Prophet Muhammad (PBUH), it is reported, said, "Acquire knowledge. It enableth its possessor to distinguish right from wrong; it lighteth the way to Heaven." He also said "With knowledge man riseth to the height of goodness and to a noble position." (15)

There are many people in this world today, as was during the time of Abraham, who do not believe that the knowledge should be shared with the poor ignorant masses of people. They believe that the knowledge should be kept in their secret society and only given to the elect and chosen few. These secret societies are like sheep, in that they cling together. In fact, in the Masonic Orders the aspirant or initiate receives a sheep skin apron called "Lambskin Apron". The fact that sheep travel in groups and cling together is not the most outstanding characteristic, because other animals also cling close together and travel in groups. (Remember Abraham was commanded to kill the ram). In examining the characteristics of the sheep we can see that the sheep is a peaceful animal. It is humble, submissive and agreeable. It has a strong social conscious. Sheep are not violent, in fact they go silently to their death. The sheep can also be understood as a symbol of a sheepish and humble people. The sheep has tremendous balance. Imam W. Deen Muhammad, a profound teacher, explained in a recent radio broadcast, that Abraham actually belonged to a sheepish society of people. He explains that Abraham belonged to a people who only desired peace and did not fight or contend with the world for progress or opportunity for progress. "So God told him (Abraham) to sacrifice the sheep...and feed it to the needy and the poor." "What is sacrifice?" he asked. "It means that you have done away with that order." The sheepish order is an order that does not trust its wisdom with the general members of the community. "The sheepish order is an order that keeps its wisdom in the ram. And its wisdom governs the order of the sheep, but through the ram. The sheep can not have that wisdom, it is only for the ram. It is only for the male, the leader in the sheepish community."

Abraham sacrificing the sheep can also be understood to mean that the human being should not become overly passive and humble. We should not become so pious that we leave the responsibility of running the world to other people. Abraham was a Muslim, he was a worker, he fought and strove hard to establish the concept of "One God." We must kill that tendency in us to become sweet sheep for slaughter. Muslims can never accept being led to the slaughter house silently. The Christian Bible presents Jesus as a meek and humble person who accepted to be persecuted and murdered without ever giving a fight. According to the Bible, Jesus said, if you are ever slapped on one cheek, turn the other so that you may be slapped on that one also. It says **"Blessed are the meek, for they shall inherit the earth."** This is not to say that Muslims are not to be forgiving and submissive. Prophet Muhammad (PBUH) and his faithful companions were tortured and persecuted for many years before the command was given to Prophet Muhammad to fight with those who fight with you. the Holy Qur'an says, **"Those who believe fight in the cause of God, and those who reject faith fight in the cause of Evil: So fight ye against the friends of Satan: feeble indeed is the cunning of Satan."** (4:76). 't also says, **"And why should ye not fight in the cause of God and of those who being weak, are ill-treated (and oppressed)?"** Allah (God) did not make us sheep, He made us human beings and we should fight falsehood with our tongues, with our heart, and with our hands. "The most excellent Jihad is that for the conquest of self." Allah wants us to be balanced, not extremist. He tells us to seek with all of our means the hereafter, but not to forget our share of this material world. The materialist loves sheepish minded people. They love people who don't want any part of this precious creation. As long as the oppressors of truth and justice can keep the people in a sheepish state of mind, they will continue to do so, while at the same time exploiting the earth of its many jewels and resources.

History of Prophet Muhammad

The history of Prophet Muhammad (PBUH) from birth to death is extremely enlightening and interesting. It reflects the power and mercy of the Creator as well as the potential of human growth and development. The history of this man serves as a model, a classic example of the ability in the human being, as ordained by Allah (God) to overcome the oppressive and destructive forces of the world. Prophet Muhammad's life illustrates to humanity the need and the ability to master one's own self, i.e. passions and desires, etc. The Prophet (PBUH) was a mortal human being first, like all other prophets. In fact, the Holy Quran says **"If there were settled on earth angels walking about in peace and quiet, we should certainly have sent them down from the heavens an angel for an apostle."** (Surah 17:95)

Prophet Muhammad is a descendant of Abraham and his wife, Hagar. It is generally understood and accepted that Prophet Muhammad (PBUH) came from the bloodline of Isma'il, Abraham's eldest son. Muhammad was born in the Holy City of Makkah around 570 A.D. His mother's name was Aminah, and his father's name was Abdullah, the son of Abdul Muttalib. Muhammad's father died about six months before he was born, and his mother died when he was only six years old. He was then placed under the care and protection of Abdul Muttalib, his grandfather after whose death his uncle, Abu Talib, took care of him. Before and during most of Muhammad's life, the people from which he was born, the Arabs, were in complete darkness (ignorance).

Arabia Before Prophet Muhammad

Prior of the advent of Prophet Muhammad (PBUH) and the message of Al-Islam, according to documented history, the Arabs were an uncivilized, ignorant and backwards people. This period in their history is known as the Jahiliya, the age of Ignorance. Although the Dark Ages occurred throughout Europe and the Middle East, it has been reported by some historians that the knowledge of civilization was more lacking in Arabia than in all other parts of the known world. Rudolph Windsor points out that "when Muhammad was born, many Arabs were still worshipping the sun, stars, spirits and idols." (From Babylon to Timbuktu, p. 45). Haykal writes, "The Arabs were happy with their paganism, contented to follow in the footsteps of their ancestors, and prepared to leave both Christians and Jews alone as long as these were not interfering with their religion. Thus, idol worship continued to flourish.

In his book The Evolution of Religion Through the Prophets, Imam Armiya Nu'Man states that "one of the major reasons that paganism flourished was because Christian and Jewish sects were warring with each other, and the Jews that were living in Yathrib (later to be renamed Medina) tolerated idol worship in order to gain trade routes." (p.11) According to Abdul A'la Maududi, at the time of the Prophet's birth darkness had covered most of the then known world. He says, "There was only a faint glimmer of learning which could hardly illumine the horizon of human knowledge....Education was a luxury meant only for the most fortunate; and education institutions there hardly existed...indeed, humanity was steeped in ignorance and superstition. Whatever light of learning there was seemed to be fighting a losing battle against the darkness prevailing all around." He continues, "In that benighted era, there was a territory--Arabia--where darkness lay heaviest and thickest."(17)

He explains that Arabia, at that time, was a country without a government. There was no law except that of the jungle. Looting, arson and murder of innocent people was the order of the day. These people worshipped stones, trees, idols and stars. They were a people of such promiscuity and lewdness that words cannot adequately describe their condition. In many cases sons married their mothers, fathers slept with their daughters. Before the revelation of the Holy Qur'an, they were very superstitious people. They spent much of their time drawing lots and reading omens. These people were so superstitious and ignorant until they built and worshipped 360 idols in the Kaaba (which was built by Prophet Abraham and his son Isma'il) one idol for each day of the year. Some of them would perform rituals, which they deemed sacred, around the Kaaba, in the nude. Even their women would become nude at the ceremony of cirumambulation of the Ka'ba. "They would stand stark naked before each other without any qualms of conscience." History reveals that they were a very silly and gangland people. Different tribes were always at daggers drawn with one another. Generation-long blood feuds began over such minor things as horse racing, grazing of cattle, and the drawing of water. Many of them were poets, their leaders were orators and warmongers. Fakir Syed Waheed Ud-Din, in his book The Benefactor points out that "the Arabs cared little for reading or writing. They were uncommonly proud, however, of their poetry, their language, and their eloquence, so much so that the rest of mankind were to them the Ajam—the dumb and speechless." The Arabs lived in cultural, scientific and spriritual darkness. They were a culturally unformed, underdeveloped people.

In the midst of all this darkness and paganism came forth a bright light. As a young man, Muhammad, like Abraham, could not accept the false worship and barbaric condition of this people. Muhammad, before becoming the last messenger of Allah (God) did not isolate himself from the challenges of society, he met and overcame them. Iman W.D. Muhammad points out that "he (Muhammad) did not run from the slum areas and their problems of alcohol, prostitution, gambling and filth. He was strong enough to live among the ignorant without falling victim to the corruption in the society, and to provide a living example of the way of life which Allah intended for human beings. He was sincere, truthful, honest, rational and upright; and he was deeply troubled by the confusion, corruption and misguided sentiments of his people." (18) This man was so truthful until his people referred to him as Al-Amin, the "Trustworthy One." He was a very hard working young man. He learned trading and commerce from his uncle and became a trader. Allama Afzalur Rahman, explains that "first he (Muhammad) went with his uncle on commercial trips to the Middle East countries, but then he began to trade on his own. He was extremely honest and fair in his dealings with all people. He lived a very quiet and peaceful life and was respected and honoured by all the people of Makkah, rich as well as poor."

Muhammad used to reflect and ponder much over the state of humanity. As he grew older, he used to go off into seclusion in the cave of Hira where he would spend days and nights thinking and meditating on the creation and the Creator. He was also seeking answers to human suffering. Maududi explains it this way: "He finds everything around him out of harmony with his soul. He retires to the hills away from the hum and drum of habitation. He spends days and nights in perfect seclusion and meditation. He fasts so that his soul and his heart may become still purer and nobler. He muses and ponders deep. He is in search of such a light which might melt away the encompassing darkness."

It was here in the cave Hira, at the age of forty, that Muhammad became Prophet Muhammad, the Seal of the Messengers of Allah (God). The Holy Qur'an calls it the "Night of Power." It is reported that one night while Muhammad was in the cave the angel Gabriel appeared to him and ordered him to "Read!" Muhammad answered "I cannot read." the angel again commanded him to "Read!" Muhammad answered "I cannot read." The third time the angel said, "Read! with the name of your Lord and Cherisher, Who created man, out of a (mere) clot of congealed blood: Proclaim! and your Lord is most bountiful, He Who taught the use of the Pen, Taught man that which he knew not." According to some reports, the angel pressed or gripped Muhammad each time he commanded him to read. (Sahih Muslim p. 97). This was the beginning of his birth as a Prophet and Messenger of Allah (God).

In reflecting on this particular event, we can see great wisdom. Here is a man, now, Muhammad, an unlettered man, a common person, who could not read into the many signs of creation, he was not able to interpret the secret operations of Creation and get the precious wisdom that lay hidden behind the physical creation. Here is a man who is being told to read, but yet could not read the secret language of the previous scriptures, could not read the divine language and the divine message that was written in scripture. Muhammad was not a member of any secret society of esoteric wisdom, he was not an "Elect of Twelve" or a "Sublime Prince of the Royal Secret." Here was a man that could not grasp fully the understanding of why his people were in such a primitive and backwards state of mind. Here was a man (Muhammad) who had a pure heart and could not accept the low life of his people, but yet he could not read the scripture and the Creation and arrive at a workable solution that would elevate his people and humanity. But because of this man's purity and sincerity, Allah, the Most High, the Merciful, blessed Muhammad with the knowledge, the insight and the ability to look at the signs in creation and get understanding and arrive at solutions. He was favored by Allah (God) and blessed with the wisdom that enabled him to read the previous scriptures and see the truth and the corruption that the hands of men had wrought. The Holy Quran tells us, concerning the creation of man, that Allah (God) said that he taught this man the nature of all things and then told him to teach what he had learned (2:30-34). Allah (God) taught Muhammad.

The Bible tells us that Adam did not come to life until the Creator breathed into him His breath of life. In other words, Adam was not alive in terms of knowing the true concept of Allah (God) and proper worship. But when Allah (God) breathed into him the breath of life, then he became alive to the true concept of Allah (God) and proper worship. The same principal was evident in the life of Abraham. As already discussed, he was not alive (aware) of the proper worship of Allah (God), although in his heart he knew that there was a Creator, and his nature told him that what his people were doing was not correct. According to history, Abraham also had to be taught the proper concept of Allah (God). The Holy Quran tells us that Abraham turned his vision to three objects for worship: first the stars, second the moon, and lastly the sun, after which he came into the true concept of God and proper worship. Prophet Muhammad (PBUH) did not read the first time or the second time, it was only after the third command was given did he "read" with the name of Allah. Muhammad had already lived a lifetime (forty years) among his people.

In the early years of his mission, Prophet Muhammad and his few followers preached the message of Al-Islam secretly for about three years. His first followers were his wife Khadijah, his friend Abu Bakr, his cousin Ali, and his freed man, Zayd. Afzalur Rahman in his "Muhammad Encyclopedia of Seerah," Vol. I, writes, "After an interval, the Revelations continued and he quietly, but steadfastly, began to preach the Doctrine of Monotheism (oneness of God) and good ways of living, to his relatives, friends and close associates. His wife, Khadijah, was the first to embrace Islam. Then his close associates, one by one, began to come into the fold of Islam: His very close friend, Abu Bakr; his slave, Zaid; his cousin, Ali; and then Othman bin Uffan, Talka, Zubau and Abdur Rahman bin Auf became Muslims. This great and noble preaching continued in secret for three years." Acording to some reports, these three years produced only forty followers and they are known as "the first and foremost." (19)

Then one day the Prophet Muhammad (PBUH) received a revelation commanding him to teach and preach the message openly to the people: **"Therefore expound openly what thou art commanded, and turn away from those who join false gods with God."** (15:94) The Prophet (PBUH) gathered his nearest relatives from the family of Quraish and invited them to the religion of Al-Islam and the Oneness of Allah (God). He said, "My Lord has commanded me to call you unto Him. Who of you then would stand by me on this matter?" No one responded positively except Ali, who said: "Prophet of Allah, I shall be your helper." After addressing his family, Muhammad directed his call to all of the people of Makkah. It is reported that one day he climbed to the top of the hill of Al Safa and called out, "O people of Quraish! Tell me, if I were to tell you that I see a cavalry on the other side of the mountain, about to attack you, would you believe me?" They answered, "Yes, for we trust you, and we have never known you to tell a lie." Muhammad said, "Know then that I am a warner and that I warn you of a severe punishment. O Banu Abd Al Muttalib! O Banu Abd Manaf! O Banu Zukrah! O Banu Taym! O Banu Makkzum! O Banu Asad! Allah (God) has commanded me to warn you, that I can guarantee to you no good on earth or in heaven unless you witness that there is no god but Allah." In another appeal to his people, he said "I invite you to these words which are very light on the tongue and very weighty in the measure: that is to bear witness that there is no god but Allah and that I am His Apostle."

The people of Makkah responded with ridicule and anger. Abu Lahab, the Prophet's uncle, was particularly harsh.

Despite the ridicule and the persecution, Prophet Muhammad continued teaching and spreading the message of Al-Islam openly. For thirteen years his primary aim was to instill in the people's mind the concept of the Oneness of Allah (Tauhid). The 112th Surah of the Holy Qur'an reads:

"Say, He is Allah, the One and Only;
God the Eternal, Absolute;
He begetteth not, or is He begotten;
And there is none like unto Him."

As Muhammad's followers increased, so did the attacks and cruelty of their persecutors. It should be noted, that although the Quraish and the people of Makkah did not like what the Prophet (PBUH) was saying, initially they dismissed him and took his message very lightly. However, as they began to realize that the Prophet (PBUH) was serious, that he was getting converts, and his message was spreading, they intensified their persecution. They decided to crush and snuff out the religion of Al-Islam. They even plotted to kill Muhammad (PBUH) on several occasions. This was very difficult because first of all, he was protected by Allah.

Another important reason was that according to the unwritten code of the Arabs, a clansman's life was sacred to the whole clan and no one "would deliberately stain his hands with the blood of a kinsman."

After a while, the Makkan leaders became so desperate and frustrated over the success of Muhammad, that they broke their own code and agreed that they would assassinate the Prophet. Learning of this vicious plot on the very night it was to be carried out, Muhammad left for Medinah. This is known as **The Hijrah** (the migration from Makkah to Medinah). This took place in the 13th year of his mission.

Allah says to the Holy Prophet:

**"Remember how the unbelievers plotted against thee,
To keep thee in bonds, or slay thee, or get thee
Out of your homes. They plot and plan, and Allah
Too, plans, but the best of Planners is Allah."**
H.Q. 8:30.

Prophet Muhammad (PBUH) asked Ali to stay in his bed until morning, so that he could pay back the valuables entrusted to him (Muhammad) by various people, and quietly left the house unnoticed by anyone. When the assassins finally arrived at the Prophet's house and found Ali in Muhammad's bed, they became very furious and even more determined to find him. So much so, that they offered a reward for his capture, dead or alive. Accompanied by his faithful companion Abu Bakr, Prophet Muhammad made it to Medinah safely. However, before arriving in Medinah, a very important event occurred en route.

The Prophet and Abu Bakr took shelter in a cave on the mountain of Thaur for three days. As they hid in the cave, the enemies approached even closer to them. Abu Bakr became greatly troubled, and said to the Prophet (PBUH), "There are only two of us and they are many. What if we are discovered?" Prophet Muhammad replied, "Fear not, there are not two of us but three, and the third amongst us is Allah (God)."

The Holy Qur'an refers to this incident in these words:

"For Allah did indeed help him when the unbelievers
Drove him out: he had no more than one companion.
They two were in the cave, and he said to his
Companion, "Have no fear for Allah is with us."
H.Q. 9:40

It is important to mention here that before the Prophet's migration to Medinah, he allowed approximately eighty of his followers to migrate to Abyssinia, which was a friendly country on the other side of the Red Sea. At that time, it was ruled by a just and trustworthy Christian King called "Negus". After hearing the message of the Qur'an, he embraced the religion of Al-Islam.

According to the history, the first thing the Prophet did upon arriving in Medinah, was to erect a Masjid (House of Worship), which today is known as **"Masjid of the Prophet"**. It is also referred to in the Holy Qur'an:

"There is a mosque (masjid) whose foundation was laid
From the first day on piety; it is more worthy of thy
Standing forth (for prayer) therein. In it are men
Who love to be purified; and Allah loveth those who
Made themselves pure." H.Q. 9:108

The second thing that the Prophet did in Medinah was to strengthen the ties of brotherhood between the immigrants from Makkah (called the **Muhajirs**), and the helpers (**Ansars**) of Medinah. The Holy Qur'an says:

"Those who believed, and adopted exile, and fought
For the faith with their properties, and their persons
In the cause of Allah, as well as those who gave them
Asylum and aid, these are all friends and protectors
One of another." H.Q. 8:72

In another effort to consolidate the positions of Muslims in Medinah, the Messenger made a treaty with the neighboring

Jewish tribes for mutual help and defense of the city.

Change in the Qiblah (Direction for Prayer)

Prophet Muhammad and his Muslim community used to face towards Jerusalem when making their prayers. Many of the Prophets and Messengers of God traveled to Jerusalem and lived there. Jerusalem was a "City of Peace" for many years, but it became materialistic. So Prophet Muhammad was yearning for a new and better direction for prayer. Allah (God) commanded him to orient himself in prayer towards the **Ka'aba**, which was built by Abraham and Isma'il. It was then revealed:

> **"We see the turning of thy face (for guidance)**
> **To the heavens: now shall we turn thee to a**
> **Qibla (direction), that shall please thee.**
> **Turn thy face in the direction of the Sacred Mosque:**
> **Wherever ye are, turn your faces in that direction."**
>
> H.Q. 2:144

The Jews in the vicinity of Medinah, at that time, became very upset; they challenged him by asserting that if he were a true Prophet, not only would he continue to pray towards Jerusalem, but would make it his home, as did some of the other prophets. Allah revealed to Muhammad the following:

> **"The fools among the people will say: 'What hath**
> **turned them from the Qibla to which they were used?'**
> **Say: To Allah belongs both East and West: He guideth**
> **Whom He will to a way that is straight."**
> H.Q. 2:142

The Prophet's Conquest of Makkah

After living in Medinah and establishing the Faith there and abroad for approximately eight years, Prophet Muhammad and many of his followers returned to the Holy City Makkah, which was still in the hands of the enemies.

By this time, however, the Muslims were large in numbers and strength, while the enemies were much smaller and weaker. "It was different now. Their name and power were already great, so none interfered with them on their march nor tried to bar their way." (20)

When Muhammad entered the City of Makkah, there was no resistance; the Makkans surrendered without a fight. The Prophet Muhammad (PBUH) did not order his followers to slaughter men, women, and children. History tells us that he announced a general amnesty for all his enemies and treated the people of Makkah with generosity and mercy. It is reported that he said, "O Men of Quraish, what do you think I am about to do with you?" They answered, "Everything good! For you are a noble brother and a noble nephew of ours." The Prophet (PBUH) then said, "Rise then, and go, you are free!"

The Prophet (PBUH), then entered the Ka'aba and destroyed all of the idols. Each time he destroyed one he would recite: **"Say, the truth is now present and falsehood must vanish."**

Once the Ka'aba was purified of all of its idols, the Prophet ordered Bilal Ibn Rabah to go on top of the Ka'aba and call the **Adhan** (the call to Prayer). Most of the people of Makkah submitted and accepted the religion of Al-Islam. This message spread throughout the whole Arabian peninsula, and people came into the faith "in crowds". Allah then revealed to Prophet Muhammad this last Surah:

> **"When comes the help of Allah, and victory,**
> **And thou dost seeth the people enter Allah's**
> **Religion in crowds;**
> **Celebrate the Praises of thy Lord, and pray**
> **For His forgiveness:**
> **For He is Oft-returning (in Grace and Mercy).**

H.Q. 110-1-3

The Prophet later returned to Medinah where he became sick. He died in the eleventh year of Hijrah (migration). This was the 23rd year of his Prophethood. May Allah's Peace and Blessings be upon him forever.

Before his death, it is reported that during his last address he said, among other things:

"All Muslims, free or enslaved, have the same rights and responsibilities. No one is higher than another unless he is higher in virtue.

O people, though an Abyssinian slave may become your Amir (Ruler), listen and obey him, as long as he executes the Book of Allah among you.

O people! Listen to what I say, and take it to heart. I leave you with the Book of Allah, and the Sunnah of His Prophet. If you follow them, you will never go astray. You must know that every Muslim is the brother of another Muslim. You are equal. You are members of one common brotherhood. It is forbidden for any of you to take from his brother save what the latter should willingly give. Do not oppress your people. O Lord! I have delivered Your Message." (21)

During the 23 years of Prophet Muhammad's life and mission, he defined the Faith and established the principle of this Religion. Through him, Allah completed and perfected the religion of Al-Islam. In that short span of time (23 years), the message of the Qur'an transformed pagan Arabia from an uncivilized and backwards society to the torchbearers of Allah's Truth. They became the leaders in science and human awareness. From that point, the Muslims revolution-ized most of the then known world. The Message of Al-Islam spread into Africa, Europe, and Asia, and started the wheels of science and civilization to begin spinning. In Africa, it complemented the many achievements that the Africans had already made. When Al-Islam came into Africa, it regenerated and reactivated the thrust for science and knowledge; it reinstated the belief in One Creator.

We find from reading the history that Prophet Muhammad placed such a high value on education that he freed unbelievers captured in battle, on the condition that they each taught ten Muslims to read and write. He made the way to knowledge easy for common people, and he made the way to economic sustenance accessible to the poor.

Imam W. Deen Muhammad pointed out that:

"Prophet Muhammad (PBUH) restored moral, intellectual, and spiritual freedom, dignity, and equality to women. He was not an Arab Nationalist, because he thought just as much of Egyptian, Ethiopian, Roman, or any other national dignity, as he did of Arab dignity." (22)

He continues, "Al-Islam is designed to appeal to our intellects so that we will be able to make the best use of our lives. Our religion is more than just a religion of faith. It is a rational religion of knowledge and logic. It is the fulfillment of the missions of all the prophets who led society to a faith that recognizes the existence of the One Creator, and the obligation of every creature to Him. The logic of Al-Islam begins with the first promise: 'I bear witness that there is no god except Allah, and Muhammad in His Servant and Messenger'." (23)

The spread of Al-Islam into Africa was not designed to establish oppressive Muslim empires, nor to destroy and rob the people of their culture and civilization, as some historians would have us to believe. The religion of Al-Islam and its true adherents never enslaved Africans or any other people. In fact, the history of Al-Islam reveals that it freed the slaves and made great African leaders.

J. A. Rogers, in his great work entitled, "World's Great Men of Color", points out that:

"With the rise of Islam, the influence of Africans in the Middle East became a more noticeable feature of the religious and cultural transition in this part of the world. The African, "Antar", is one of the many Black heroes who emerged at the time a new and dynamic religion, Islam, was challenging the social order of the day. He became, and remains, one of the great heroes of his religion." (24)

He also points out, for example, that Bilal Ibn Rabah, who he describes as a tall, gaunt, bush-haired Black Ethiopian slave, was among the first of those to accept the faith of Al-Islam. He was freed by a Muslim companion of the Prophet (PBUH), Abu Bakr, and was chosen by the Prophet to be the first **Muezzin** (Caller to Prayer), and the Treasurer of Islam.

J. A. Rogers tells us about "Ibrahim Al-Makdi", whom he describes as "Islam's Greatest Songster, and Caliph of Bagdad" (799 A.D.). "Ibrahim, as a young man, was carefully tutored in science, poetry, dialectics, and other branches of Moslem culture." (25)

He then turns our attention to Malik Ambar (1548-1628), a brilliant Military leader and Statesman of India. Mr. Rogers writes in his Reference that, "Slavery was never a barrier to an ambitious slave, Black or White, under Mohammedan rule. Mahmud of Ghazni, the greatest of the Mohammaden rulers of India, was born of slave parentage." (26)

Yakub Al-Mansur (1149-1199), another shining example, was one of the great and most powerful Moorish rulers of Spain. He was also one of the most enlightened, most just, and magnanimous. "Like nearly all of the rulers of Morocco, he had a Negro strain." By the influence of Al-Islam, we learn that under the leadership of Askia the Great (1538), the Songhai Empire flourished until it became one of the richest of that time.

Timbuktu became one of the world's greatest centers of science and learning. Sunni Ali, who came before Askia, was the founder of Timbuktu. Mr. Rogers writes: "Of the several Negro kingdoms that rose in West Africa between the eleventh and sixteenth centuries, the most notable was Songhai."(27) Sunni Ali lead this empire to the heights of splendor, power, and prosperity.

Dr. Edward Blyden, in his book _Christianity, Islam, and the Negro Race_, writes:

"After the first conquest of the Muslims in North Africa, their religion advanced southwards into the continent, not by arms, but by schools, books, and Mosques. They could not have brought a force sufficient to subjugate the people, for they had to deal with large, powerful, and energetic tribes...you can understand why it is then that Islam has such a hold upon the African tribes who have embraced it...The Faith becomes a part of their nationality, and is entwined with their affections. Arguments from outsiders have no weight with them. There are names and phrases which have such effect upon their minds and so thrill them as supersede and transcend all argument...that theory, which attributes the success of Islam in Africa to what are frequently denounced as the sensual aspects of the religion, is based upon ignorance, not only of the system, but of the elementary facts of human nature. No religion existing so powerfully holds sway over 200 million people of all races and climates for more than a thousand years which appealed chiefly to the lower passion...as Mohammadanism and learning to the Negro were coeval. No sooner was he taught to read, the importance of knowledge was impassed to him." (28)

In discussing the contribution of Al-Islam throughout the world, Imam W. Deen Muhammad, in the book, _Prayer and Al-Islam_, states:

"It was through the message of Al-Islam that the Western World received the light of civilization and the foundations foremost in its own artistic and scientific achievements.

Through Islamic society, the Western World received knowledge of 'the scientific method' which outlines a systematic and conclusive procedure for examining nature, and for conducting scientific and social experiments. This achievement alone has been hailed as one of the greatest in World history. It was also this society which developed great universities at Basrah, Kufah, Baghdad, Cairo, and Cordoba, over one hundred years before any such developments in Europe. These learning centers drew the best students from throughout Asia, Africa, and Europe."

"Muslims invented the mathematical sciences of Algebra and Trigonometry. In Physics, they invented the pendulum, and did great works in the field of optics. They developed an extensive knowledge of Astronomy, built numerous observatories, and constructed many astronomical instruments which are still in use. They calculated the angle of the ecliptic and the procession of the equinoxes. In medicine they studied Physiology and Hygiene, and many of their methods of treatment are still in use today. Their surgeons were proficient in the use of anesthetics, and they performed some of the most difficult operations known." (29)

Dr. Maurice Bucaille in his book, The Bible, The Qur'an, and Science, after stating certain facts about Al-Islam, writes:

"We must note here that the above facts concerning Islam are not generally known in the West. It is hardly surprising, when we consider the way so many generations in the West were instructed in the religious problems facing humanity and in what ignorance they were kept about anything related to Islam. The use of such terms as "Mohammadan religion" and "Mohammadans" has been instrumental—even to the present day—in maintaining the false notion that beliefs were involved that were spread by the work of a man among which God (in the Christian sense) had no place." (30)

Dr. Muhammad Hamidullah in his book, Introduction To Islam, points out that the Religion of Al-Islam made major contributions in the field of Law. He states:

"In its comprehensive character, Legal Science developed among Muslims very early. They were the first in the world to entertain the thought of an abstract science of law, distinct from the codes of the general laws of the country.." (31)

Fundamental Principles of Al-Islam

As Muslims, we are to have a universal and holistic view of man and the world. Al-Islam is a comprehensive religion, in that it addresses every aspect of human life. The human being, as mentioned earlier, begins his growth through the five senses, which are very important. They, in many ways, serve as a foundation from which we support ourselves. Our religion (Al-Islam) consists of five basic, but essential principles, namely:

1. *To bear witness that there is no god except One Allah (God), the Eternal and Absolute; and that Prophet Muhammad Ibn Abdullah is His Last Prophet and Messenger.*

2. *To make Prayer five times a day.*

3. *To pay Charity.*

4. *To Fast during the month of Ramadan.*

5. *To make Hajj (Pilgrimage) to the Holy House in Makkah (once in a lifetime).*

It is reported that one day while Prophet Muhammad (PBUH) was sitting with some of the Believers and Companions, there appeared before them a man whose clothes were "exceedingly white and whose hair was exceedingly black". He walked up and sat down by the Prophet (PBUH) placing his knees against the Prophet's knees, with his hand on his thigh and said,
"O Muhammad, tell me about Al-Islam. "The Prophet said, "Islam is to testify that there is no god but Allah, and Muhammad is the Messenger of Allah; to perform the prayers; to pay the Zakat (charity); to Fast in the month of Ramadan; and to make the Pilgrimage to the House (Ka'aba) if you are able to do so." He said, "You have spoken rightly!".
(Forty Hadith)

-33-

When we consciously acknowledge ourselves as Muslims and openly testify that there is no god but Allah and Muhammad is His Messenger, we take on the responsibility of living in accord with the Word of Allah (Al-Qur'an) and the Sunnah (Traditions) of Prophet Muhammad (PBUH). We are actually telling the world that man is not God, nor any of man's inventions. We are also letting the world know and reminding ourselves that Prophet Muhammad is not the son of God, or "God manifest", but that he is a human Messenger of Allah. In taking the Shahadah (declaration of faith), we are acknowledging and proclaiming the Oneness of the Creator.

This world has advanced the lie that Jesus Christ is Allah (God), and has caused many good people to go astray from the pure teachings that he taught. In fact, in one of their "secret orders" called "Freemasonry", the instructor of the meetings is called "Worshipful Master". The corrupt leaders of this world has caused us to bow down (in our actions and thoughts) and worship their gods as the real God. The Muslim only worships Allah, the Most High, the Creator of all things, and we fear Him, alone. This is why the corrupt and deceitful rulers in this land and abroad don't want this message spread among the masses of the people, particularly among the ex-slaves, the African-Americans.

What the Muslim says, however, to America, Europe, Russia, and the other world powers, is that "You don't scare us. You don't really have any power compared to the Lord of all the worlds!"

The Holy Qur'an says: **"Not one of the beings in the heavens and the earth but must come to Allah, Most Gracious, as a servant."** (H.Q. 19:93)

Allah is One, Absolute. He has no partners or associates. This first Principle of Al-Islam is the most important Principle of the faith. We must be sincere and truthful!

As Muslims, we also have six fundamental beliefs, called "Articles of Faith". They are:

1. *Belief in the Oneness of Allah (H.Q. 112)*
2. *Belief in all of the Prophets (3:84)*
3. *Belief in all the Revealed Books (4:136)*
4. *Belief in the Angels (2:177)*
5. *Belief in the Hereafter and Judgement (2:4)*
6. *Belief in Divine Ordinance or Pre-Determination (47:22)*

Allah tells us in Al-Qur'an that we must believe in these Articles of Faith and conduct ourselves accordingly. "...Whoso disbelieve in Allah, and His angels, and His Scriptures, and His Messengers, and the Last Day, he verily has wandered far astray". (H.Q. 4:136)

We should study these principles or articles so that we can better understand them. The study of these principles is called **Aqidah.**

Imam W. Deen Muhammad, in summarizing the Articles of Faith, explains:

"The fundamental principles of Al-Islam are the most important things in a Muslim's life. We are not to look for ways to modify the Principles of Al-Islam to justify unlawful and unnatural practices. We are to alter our attitudes and practices to conform to Islamic Principles...

"**Faith in Allah** means that we believe in Him and trust Him over everything else.

"**Belief in Allah's Prophets** means that we accept all of His Prophets, as well as the fact that Prophet Muhammad (PBUH), the most noble and honorable of all creatures, is Allah's Last Prophet, and our leader and example, who we obey and follow.

"**Belief in the Books** that the Prophets brought means that we are to question all books under the light of what is revealed in the Holy Qur'an.

"**Belief in Allah's Angels** means that we must seek to understand the phenomena operating between our vision of reality and the truth that Allah has revealed.

"Belief in the Divine Ordinance means we believe that Allah has law operating throughout creation, and in every phase of our lives, to give us the benefits of our good deeds and the consequences of our bad ones. It means we believe that we cannot escape the Justice of Allah.

"Belief in the Day of Resurrection (Judgement Day) means we believe that this scheme of creation is on time and for a purpose. It is a training ground, a testing place where we prove ourselves worthy of reaching a higher stage in the fulfillment of our aspirations. We believe that Allah will provide a new creation where we will have an opportunity to realize the fullness of our good aspirations. Because of this, we should always have hope and we should never despair." (32)

The Light Of Allah

> **"Allah is the light of the heavens and the earth. The parable of His light is as if there were a niche, and within it a lamp; the lamp enclosed in glass: the glass as if it were a brilliant star lit from a blessed tree, an olive, neither of the East nor of the West.** H.Q. 24:35

Allah (God) has power over all things at all times. His Truth, Wisdom, and Power is not limited to either the East or the West. His Light is not confined to just spiritual or material operations. Allah's Truth is not bound to the past, but it is universal, for all times. Prophet Muhammad (PBUH), brought a universal message. One of the Attributes of Allah is As-Samad (The Eternal). The Creator never loses one ounce of His Knowledge and Power; He is All-Wise, Most Merciful, Most Gracious, Ever-Present. Just as Allah blessed the deserving people in the past, He can and does bless truthful, sincere people today! The light of the Qur'an has shone forth into the Western hemisphere.

According to the Bible, Jesus said, **"For as the lightning cometh out of the East, and shineth even unto the West;**

so shall also the coming of the Son of Man be." (Matt. 25:27)

In the history of Prophet Muhammad we learn that he had a vision, and that in that vision he traveled from Makkah westward to Jerusalem (West), where he prayed with Abraham, Moses, and Jesus. (This event is called Al-Isra). The Holy Qur'an says, "**Glory to Allah Who did take His servant for a journey by night from the Sacred Mosque to the Farthest Mosque, whose precincts He did Bless in order that we might show him some of our signs.**" (H.Q. 17:1)

Some people understand this event in the Prophet's life to be the fulfillment of the "Son of Man coming from the East and going to the West". Such persons are entitled to that particular understanding. However, wisdom dictates that it is intelligent and proper to view history as it is, and to also see how it connects and relates to current or present situations and events. In other words, we are to learn from history what to do and what not to do in the present and the future, and to also draw from the experiences of other people.

Allah tells us in the Holy Qur'an to "**Travel through the land and see what was the fate of those who came before us**". Both the Bible and the Qur'an relates to us parables and stories about how Allah (God) bestowed His Mercy upon a particular people and also how He brought His Wrath down on others. Allah tells us in the Qur'an that Prophet Muhammad was a mercy to all of humanity. As Muslims, we should learn these truths and marvel over the greatness of Allah as it relates to the events of the past. But as God-conscious, right-minded people, we should also look for the manifestation of His Power and Mercy in this day and time, particularly in our lives here in America, in the West.

The African-American Slave Experience

Approximately four centuries ago, the African-American people were kidnapped from their motherland and their people. Although in some cases they were sold by their leaders, the fact remains that an overwhelming number of Africans were kidnapped by the European and American invaders. Millions of Africans were killed trying to resist the invaders, but because the Europeans had greater weapons and were more deceitful than the Africans, they were able to overpower them, bound their necks, feet, and hands in chains, and force them into the slaveships. According to some reports, they were packed in like sardines.

J. C. DeGraft-Johnson writes in his book, African Glory, "It is little wonder then, that slaves not only died from physical ill-treatment, but also from grief, rage, and despair. Some undertook hunger strikes; some undid their chains and hurled themselves on the crew in futile attempts at insurrection. In order to combat grief and melancholy among the slaves, it became the custom to have them on deck once a day and force them to dance, but even in these cases, many a slave took the opportunity to jump overboard, uttering cries of triumph as he cleared the vessel and disappeared below the surface. There are indeed limits to the degradation the human spirit will endure."

The crossing of the Atlantic Ocean from Africa to America is often referred to as "The Middle Passage". The number of deaths incurred ranges in the vicinity of 15 to 20 percent, and although it is difficult to really determine the actual number of slaves who died during the Middle Passage, it is documented that on one occasion, that out of 7,904 slaves, 2,053 slaves died. It should be noted that the Middle Passage generally lasted fifty days.

Generally speaking, it is not in the power of human imagination to picture a situation more dreadful and disgusting than the European Slave Trade. Imagine human beings being stacked in the bottom of ships chained together. As one Captain of a slave ship stated, "They were as comfortable as a man might be in his coffin." We should reflect deeply on this, because it was at this particular time that the process of dehumanization began to take place in the African-American's life! These were human beings, many of which were Muslims. Many of the slaves believed that there was no god but Allah, and that Prophet Muhammad (PBUH) is His Last Messenger.

According to a surgeon who was on board of one of the slave ships, "While they (slaves) were in this situation, my profession requiring it, I frequently went down among them, till at length, their apartments became so extremely hot as to be sufferable for just a very short time. But the excessive heat was not the only thing that rendered their situation intolerable. The deck, that is the floor of their rooms, was so covered with the blood and mucous which had proceeded from them in consequence of the flux, that it resembled a slaughterhouse...Numbers of the slaves had fainted, they were carried on deck, where several of them died, and the rest were with difficulty, restored. It nearly proved fatal to me, also."

Once the ships arrived in America, the Caucasian slave master established the institution of slavery in America. Many of the African slaves were killed outright, if they were deemed "unfit" for labor. Here in America, we were stripped of our language, our culture, our name, our religion, and we were robbed of the knowledge of self and others. The Caucasian slave master reduced us to the level of animals and would mate our slave parents, separate them, then raise the child with a slave mentality. They forced the African--American slaves to work from sun up to sun down in the blistering heat and the freezing cold. The basic and most important unit of any society, the family, was broken up, divided, and dispersed throughout America. Mind you, most of these cruelties were done in the name of God and the Bible. So-called Christian ministers would justify our enslavement as a "curse". They taught that we were decendants of Ham, who was cursed by his father Noah (according to the Bible).

The African-American slave was deprived and denied education. If a slave was caught reading a book, he could be killed on the spot, at the very least, he was horse-whipped. It is documented that the slave masters would tie one of our fore-parents to a tree and make his slave brother whip him until he became unconscious. The slave masters were so cruel, according to some reports, that if it was believed that the slaves were about to rebel, a pregnant woman would be tied to a tree, and the slave master would cut her stomach open causing the baby to fall to the ground, after which the slave master would crush it with his feet.

The slave master was so brutal and barbaric that mobs of them would gather together to view with delight, the lynching and burning of a human being, whose skin happened to have been so-called "Black". The Caucasian white supremacist set himself up as God, dictating to our foreparents what names they should have, what foods they should eat, where and when to relieve their waste. Worst still, they brainwashed us thoroughly until today, 1985, we still fear and worship an image of them as God. The institution of slavery reduced us (African-Americans) to the level of pagans, infidels, and idolaters. The light of our minds were brutally put out by the vicious and cowardly slave masters. (It is important to note that "African-Americans" were taken from a civilized and established society—a society that had governments, law, science, fear of God, learning institutions. It was only after the Caucasian Christians invaded Africa that they, African nations, began to decline).

The cruel system of slavery, and racism put us in mental, moral, spiritual, and cultural darkness (ignorance). David Walker (1829), in his "Appeal" proclaimed, "Yet the American minister sent out missionaries to convert the heathen, while they kept us and our children sunk at their feet in the most abject ignorance and wretchedness that ever a people was afflicted with since the world began." Again, after we were forced into such a pitiful condition, the slave masters very deceitfully planted unnatural slavemaking ideas into the slaves' mind. These ideas shackled their mental development, thereby causing them to grope in mental darkness. After the slaves were freed and allowed to read the Bible and attend Church, the slave master made sure that the ex-slaves attended churches in which a blonde haired, blue eyed Caucasian image of Jesus was before them. The slave master placed before the slaves and ex-slaves a false god to worship. Since the so-called image of God looked like the slave master, then subconsciously, our foreparents viewed the slavemaster as being exclusively of the family of God. Therefore, many of them feared to rise up and fight the Caucasian slave master. That image and concept of God served as a powerful doctrine to keep us (African-Americans) bound in fear, mental and spiritual darkness.

The institution of slavery, with its ideology of black inferiority and white superiority, caused us to dislike our very color, our features. It caused us to love Caucasian and hate ourselves. Are we not worthy of Allah's (God's) intervention and mercy? Imam W. Deen Muhammad stated, "They skillfully severed from our minds those functions of mental and spiritual development which classify a physical body as a man or "human".

In a lecture delivered in East Orange, New Jersey (1984), Imam Muhammad reminded the audience that we (African—Americans) did not come to America as willing travelers; he stated, "Some things have to be remembered and not forgotten, and the fact of our folks being brought here by force—some of us act like we had a conference, like the Blacks had a conference and they sat down and decided to come to America, the land of plenty. It didn't happen that way. The White slave masters had a conference and they decided to take us by force and bring us here and put us in this situation...We were cut off from the natural life line of the African people by the slave masters."

The history of the African-American people as slaves, both physically and mentally verifies the fact that, we needed Divine intervention. By virtue of our suffering here in America, we are worthy to be favored by Allah to be the torchbearer of His religion of Al-Islam. We are worthy by virtue of our sincerity and oppression. Why oppression?

Because the Qur'an gives guidance to man so that he may be elevated to his dignified role as a truthful and just Khalifah (ruler) and to keep him on the path of proper worship. Those who are in most need of guidance and enlightenment are those who are oppressed, ignorant, despised, and rejected.

As we have already discussed, the Holy Qur'an and Prophet Muhammad (PBUH) came to a mentally oppressed and backwards people. Prophet Muhammad is called an "unlettered" or an uneducated man from among an uneducated people. Furthermore, if this world can claim that God intervened when the Hebrews were in bondage in Egypt, why shouldn't He intervene in our affairs?

Let the record show that first, as the religion of Al-Islam came into Arabia and civilized those backward pagan Arabs and caused them to become dignified people; and from there Al-Islam came into Africa and regenerated the Africans, dignified them, guided them to the proper worship of One Allah (God); Al-Islam has come to the West, to an ignorant, backwards, and oppressed people. It has come to a people who are spiritual, who love and fear God in their hearts, although they worship a false image of God.

Abraham, as already mentioned, had the wrong idea of Allah (God), but his heart was right and pure. The slave master and their children feared, and fear, the presence of true Al-Islam among the African-American people because they know that it will give us true freedom and they will not be able to use and manipulate us as dumb cattle any longer. In an effort to stop the light "from shining out of the Fast even unto the West," and prevent the oppressed masses from getting the pure light of Al-Islam, they created all kinds of false images and ideas of Al-Islam and spread them through the media in hopes that we will latch on to a polluted form of Al-Islam. Al-Islam will give us culture, economic, and political dignity. It enables the human being to reach his full potential as a human being.

A Brief History of Al-Islam in America

It is difficult to pinpoint exactly when the religion of Al-Islam came to America because, according to some reports, some of the slaves were Muslims, and they managed to pass certain aspects of the religion along with their offspring. It is evident, however, that that would be short lived. The oppressors and conspirators, understanding the power of the Qur'an and the religion of Al-Islam, feared its spread among the oppressed African-Americans. Therefore, in an effort to stop us from coming into the light of Al-Islam, they concocted a false religion and put the name "Islam" on it. The deceivers, realizing that the hand of time would eventually bring us in contact with the pure and perfect religion of Allah, Al-Islam, designed various schemes, plots and traps to divert our interest and acceptance of Al-Islam.

Approximately thirteen years after the slaves supposedly received their freedom by "The Emancipation Proclamation", an organization called the **"Ancient Arabic Order of Nobles of the Mystic Shrine"** was established. It is alleged that this organization was created in Makkah, by Ali, the Prophet Muhammad's cousin, in the year of Hijrah (The Prophet's Migration to Medinah). It is further alleged that a man by the name of William J. Florence, a 33rd degree Mason, while on a visit to Arabia, was initiated in a Temple of the Mystic Shrine. In 1871, he brought the "secret work" of Shriners to America, and placed it in the hands of a Dr. Walter M. Fleming, who, along with other Masons, established its first Temple in New York, called "Mecca Temple".

One of the objects of this organization is to give the appearance of Al-Islam, but not to actually practice the religion. According to a document obtained from the Library of Congress, entitled <u>Ancient Arabian Order of the Nobles of Mystic Shrine: Its Origin and History</u>, it states, "Their ostensible object is to increase the faith and fidelity of all true believers in Allah (whose name be exalted)." The secret and real purpose can only be made known to those who have encircled the Mystic Shrine according to the instruction in The Book of the Constitution and the Regulations of the Imperial Council. The Shriners' Ritual states, "Those of the members of the Masonic Order who desire to advance and gain admission in this sublime Rite of the Mystic Shrine are required to take a solemn vow that they will redouble their courage, zeal and determination to defend and advocate the Christian religion."

One author wrote "If children can play cops and robbers, then the Masons can play Muslims and Infidels!" The Shriners degree is considered the "Playhouse of Masonry".

As I will point out in a subsequent chapter, the Shriners learned some of the language of the Qur'an (Arabic), some history of Prophet Muhammad (PBUH), some of the rituals, and dress in the garments of Eastern Muslims. I believe that the Shriners Order was instituted to impart some profound truths to its initiates, while at the same time, attempting to discredit the purity of Al-Islam. In an article which appeared in the April 2, 1984 issue of A.M. Journal, entitled, "Know Difference Between Muslim and Devil's Dupe", it was reported that Imam W. Deen Muhammad said, "Even Shriners and Masons use Qur'anic terminology. Though they do a great service in society, no matter how nice they are, we still condemn them using terminology of Al-Islam on that which is not Al-Islam.

Master Fard Muhammad

In the year 1930, approximately sixty-seven years after the Emancipation Proclamation, and fifty-nine years after the creation of the Ancient Arabic Order of the Nobles of the Mystic Shrine in America, a man calling himself Master W. F. Muhammad, appeared in Detroit, Michigan, and began preaching in the slums of that city a doctrine which he called "Islam". This is not to say, however, that there were not others who came before Fard with the pure message of the Qur'an, but they did not have the same impact as Fard. He formed an organization called "The Lost Found Nation of Islam In North America".

For about three and a half years he preached that White people were a "race of devils", and "the Black man was God", and that we (African-Americans), "were decendants of Muslims and of a tribe called 'Shabazz'."

On page 108 of the book, "Message to the Black Man in America" by the Hon. Elijah Muhammad, it is reported that this mystic man Fard Muhammad, said that the Black man was "the writers of the Bible and Qur'an". He taught that the Caucasian people were grafted and made by the Black man. Those of us who know the old teachings, know that we were taught that a Black man named "Yakub made the White man and taught him how to lie, steal, rule, and master the Black man". Fard said that he came from Arabia by himself to seek and to save that which was lost (the African-American). He said that his mother was a pure Causcasian, and his father was an original Black man, who was a God. Let us reflect on this point for a moment because it reveals some basic contradictions and ideas that are not only un-Islamic, but are considered one fo the worst sins one could commit in Al-Islam.

Fard Muhammad taught Elijah Muhammad and many others in the 1930's that he was the "Mahdi" (Messiah), the Christ, A Prophet, and alluded to the idea that he was God. On page 17 of Elijah Muhammad's book Message To The Black Man, he writes, "I asked him (Fard Muhammad) 'Who are you and what is your real name?' He said, 'My name is Mahdi; I am God'." The Holy Qur'an says, **"Who doth more wrong than such as invent a false god against Allah?"** (H.Q.19:15)

The Mystic Fard said that his father was an original Black god and he mated with a White woman so that he, Fard Muhammad would be born of both Black and White. He reasoned that this would allow him to go among the Caucasians and the African-Americans without being discovered or recognized. (Mind you, this man is supposed to be God). He used the language of the Bible which says that "He came like a thief in the night." According to the teachings of Fard, he was the greatest god there ever was, yet he was born of a Caucasian woman. He taught that one god created the heavens and the earth, another one created the moon.

He claimed that there were twenty four scientists, (twelve major and twelve minor ones) who controlled the weather and the seasons. He called this teaching Islam. According to the lessons, W. F. Muhammad said that there never was a god as great as himself, because he had all of the wisdom of the previous gods. He had the knowledge of the twenty-four scientists, plus what his father had taught him. He professed to have the power to control the elements. He claimed that he was a Muslim and that he was teaching Islam. However, Allah tells us in the Holy Qur'an, that He was never born! That He always existed. The 112th Chapter of the Holy Qur'an clearly states:

"He is Allah, The One, The Only.
God, The Eternal, The Absolute;
He begetteth not, nor is He begotten;
And there is none like unto Him."

How could a man, having knowledge of this Chapter, and the Qur'an in general, ever suggest that he is God and was born from God? That is no different than what the Christians say about Jesus.

Fard Muhammad taught racism and called it "Islam". First of all he said that all White people were born devils. He said that his mother was a White woman but not a devil. Although he called the Caucasians Devils, and preached what appeared to be open racism against Caucasians, if we scrutinize and examine some of the things that he taught, we will see that he also taught White supremacy.

For example, he said that we (African-Americans) made the Caucasians and taught him how to be a devil. If we taught them how to be devils, then we must be responsible for all of the hell they have raised on this earth. Fard Muhammad looked just like a straight-haired, sharp-featured, brown-eyed Caucasian. He did not look like us, yet he claimed that we "were the Original man, the owner, the maker, the cream of the Planet Earth, God of the Universe". After telling us all these great things about ourselves, he turns around, with his white looking complexion, and says that he is greater than all the other Black gods that came before him and that he is the wisest one among us, therefore we should worship him as God. (Most of the African-Americans were already worshipping a Caucasian image—identified as Jesus, therefore it was easy to accept another Caucasian image). He didn't stop there with the insults, he said that our kinky hair was unnatural (we were already told by the American Caucasians that our black skin, kinky hair, and broad features were a curse on us). He taught that our hair was originally straight like our eyelashes.

After teaching for three and a half years, he left. Before leaving in 1933, he taught the Honorable Elijah Muhammad (whose name was Elijah Poole), and gave him the symbolic teachings and instructed Elijah to teach the masses of Blacks that if they would accept him (Fard) as their Saviour, and Elijah Muhammad as his Messenger, they would obtain "money, good homes, and friendship in all walks of life". Under the leadership of Elijah Muhammad, the Nation of Islam grew and prospered for forty years, teaching that God came in the Person of Master Fard Muhammad, a man, and that the Hon. Elijah Muhammad was the last Messenger of God.

It should be noted, however, that Elijah Muhammad did not start this organization, he did not originate the teachings, he was a descendant of slaves like the majority of African-Americans. He only knew what Fard taught him, and because he was faithful and determined, he preached hard for about forty-five years.

Through his efforts, and the efforts of his followers, the so-called Nation of Islam grew and attracted hundreds of thousands of African-Americans. In many ways it helped the African-American people. The teachings of the Nation of Islam gave many of us a sense of dignity and self-worth, but it also gave us a false image of the true religion of Al-Islam. Although we had the Holy Qur'an, and we were told to respect it because it was the Pure Revelation from Allah (God), we were taught that another book would come and replace the Qur'an. In fact, much of the Qur'anic language and verses were used to justify the teachings. But in the Nation of Islam we were taught that God is a man, a human being (See Message to the Blackman). Most of the teachings were symbolic and were made up of a number of philosophies.

Under the leadership of the Honorable Elijah Muhammad, the so-called Nation of Islam made great achievements. Those who followed him were given a sense of pride and dignity in their Blackness. They were taught and practiced self-respect. We were taught to be clean and always conscious of our physical appearance. Under the leadership of Elijah Muhammad emphasis was put on moral decency, truthfulness, love of self. We were taught to "do for self", and made many material accomplishments in America. Land was purchased, buildings were constructed, local businesses were opened, international trade was established through the hard labor of the Hon. Elijah Muhammad and his followers. The downtrodden, despised, and ignorant rejects of society were cleaned up and given hope and confidence.

Although many major accomplishments were made under the teachings of the Nation of Islam, we cannot use those accomplishments as the criterion for determining if in fact Fard Muhammad and Elijah Muhammad taught true Al-Islam, nor can we use them as a criterion for determining if the teachings of the once Nation of Islam was/is the answer for the Bilalian (African-American) people and humanity at large. The physical accomplishments and teachings of the once Nation of Islam cannot be used as a criterion any more than the physical accomplishments of Communism, Capitalism, Socialism, Christianity, or any other philosophy or ideology.

There are many doctrines that have helped humanity make physical and natural progress. So if we only view and judge their material achievements, then the same conclusion can be drawn. The communist can jump up and say "Communism is the answer because it led us to material success". Adherents to the capitalist doctrine can claim the same. Therefore, it is foolish and outright ignorant to claim that Fard Muhammad is God simply because he brought a mixed ideology that helped give the "Blackman" a sense of pride and self-respect. No! No! We must look into the language of the doctrine itself, into the concepts and ideas so that we may determine if the content is true to the label. The content of the once Nation of Islam was racism, white supremacy, and dark symbolism, but the label was Islam. Fard said, "Islam is mathematics, and mathematics is Islam." Mathematics is the science or art of symbols and figures. Firgures and symbols are not the reality, but are tools that can lead to reality or error, light or darkness. Al-Islam is not a religion of symbols and figures, it is The Reality, the Qur'an is The Light, and Allah is the only Reality!

Some argue that what Fard did was absolutely and vitally necessary because we African-Americans were so ignorant that we had to be gradually brought to the light of Al-Islam. That may be true, but there was no guarantee that by his methods we would come to the light. He actually experimented with us like guinea pigs. The proof that his method was not the proper method is seen in the fact that the new and current leader of the once Nation of Islam (now the American Muslim Mission), Imam Warith Deen Muhammad, rejected Fard Muhammad and his teachings, and has successfully, by the power of Allah (God), led this community to the true light of Al-Islam. In fact, Fard Muhammad, himself, asked the question, "What means and methods must be used to remove all poison (low morals) and rust (ignorance) from the said worst ones?"

Our growth into the light of truth is a gradual process. Allah tells us in the Qur'an that he raises us degree by degree, stage by stage. The Holy Qur'an, itself, was revealed in stages over a period of twenty-three years (25:32). Allah says, "There are signs in the creation for those who reflect." (30:20-22)

In reflecting on the physical creation, we observe that the sun does not first suddenly spring up, but it gradually rises in the east giving our eyes time to adjust to its brilliant rays. Our growth from the womb to the grave is also a gradual process which Allah set into motion.

The Plot of Fard Muhammad

According to both the Qur'an and the Bible, Satan said that he would approach the human being "from before him and behind him, from his left, and from his right". Just as man observes creation and learns from its various signs how to advance humanity, corrupt and wicked people also observe creation and use its signs and wisdom to manipulate humanity. According to the Holy Qur'an, Iblis had become the leader amongst the Angels. He is a knowledgeable creature, a creature of "fire" (wisdom). The Jahcubite Conspirators, in observing the physical creation and seeing that the sun as it rises, its light is mixed with darkness of the night during its dawning. In observing this natural phenomenon, they arrive at the conclusion that truth (light) can be mixed with falsehood (darkness). Allah says in the Holy Qur'an that "the sincere are guided aright by His signs, and the wicked are led further astray". It also says, "Cover not Truth with falsehood." (2:42)

Fard Muhammad mixed truth with falsehood. He understood the signs in the creation to the extent that he was able to apply it on a "spiritually dead" people. He raises and teaches us gradually by giving us the light of truth as he decides it is necessary at a particular time in our growth and development.

The American government allowed Fard's teachings to grow in America among the ex-slaves because they realized that he was working on behalf of their interest and that he was blinding us to the true religion of Al-Islam. Imam W. Deen Muhammad pointed out in 1983, at the American Muslim Mission Convention in Georgia, that "They didn't want this Black man to be free and they knew if we learned of our Islamic memory and how powerful it is in our genes because of our parents, the slave fathers and mothers being Muslims, if we learned of that, they knew that many of us would turn to Al-Islam because many of us came from that ancestry, and the tendency to go back is in the genes. They know that!... So they let Fard come over here and corrupt the Religion, put it under false names, give it false identity, mess it up so that when you hear the real religion, you won't want it!"

It should be very clear that Fard Muhammad worked against the religion of Al-Islam and he used Elijah Muhammad and his followers to do the work. Imam W. Deen Muhammad explained that, "We believed him (Fard) because he was White, and because he spoke convincingly and put God on his teachings. But now that we look back at that, and we look at it, we see that the man was really laughing at us, playing with us and shackling us so that he could demonstrate his genius—not to us—but to the world that knew what he was doing. He did not demonstrate his genius to us. We were the dumb victims, we were gullible fish, swallowing everything he said without questioning it. We didn't see the reality; it was only those people in the esoteric circles of religious sciences, Masons, Shriners, secret orders of the religious world of the oriental societies—they could look at what he was doing and see wisdom and genius in it...We were the victims of it. If Allah (God) hadn't blessed me to see, you would be in the same shape now, and our people would be fixed in the same mold of unreality that the Jacobites put the Europeans in."

He Was Born For The Mission

In 1975, when the Honorable Elijah Muhammad, who represented the teachings of Fard Muhammad for over forty years, died, Allah blessed us the next day with our leader Imam Warith Deen Muhammad, a true Muslim and follower of Prophet Muhammad (PBUH). He was born, groomed and prepared for the the mission. Allah blessed us with a leader who has insight into the symbolic teachings of Fard Muhammad and the Bible. This man, by the Mercy of Allah, has pulled away the "dark clouds of symbolism" so that the "bright light" of the Holy Qur'an could shine forth into our minds.

We who follow this leader, declare along with the other one billion Muslims throughout the world, that the Holy Qur'an is the Last, Complete and Perfect Revelation revealed by Allah (God), the Most Merciful, Most Gracious, All Powerful, All Wise Creator of the Heavens and the Earth. The One who has no beginning or ending, never tires, never sleeps, is at all times in control of His Creation, the One who created everything in existence! We bear witness openly that "There is no god but Allah, and Prophet Muhammad Ibn Adullah is His Last Messenger!

Upon coming into leadership, the sincere and faithful Imam W. Deen Muhammad began toppling the idols that were in the "Temple" of our minds. All of the false gods of Black supremacy were destroyed! Single-handedly, relying only on the Light of the Holy Qur'an, and the power of Allah, he destroyed the big idol of Fard Muhammad, and exposed his tricks and schemes. After doing this, like Prophet Muhammad (PBUH), Imam Muhammad ordered Bilal to "go on top of the Kaaba and make the Call to Prayer." Imam W. Deen Muhammad instituted the Islamic practice of Prayer. However, before doing this, he granted a period of amnesty to all the criminals (criminals here means those who committed so-called crimes as they were defined by the Nation of Islam at that time).

Reflect, here are a people (African-Americans), who were kidnapped from their native land and people, and brought to America and made slaves, reduced to the level of animals, and denied the opportunity to think like human beings and cultivate human and family life. Imagine that from among a people who were made to hate themselves and love others, a people who were used by the manipulators of this world, put into the "firery furnace" of hate and oppression, that a leader is born declaring that there is but One Allah (God), and that Prophet Muhammad is His Messenger, and that the religion of Al-Islam is the natural religion of all humanity and the answer to all ills.

Allah has blessed African-American people in general, and the former followers of the Hon. Elijah Muhammad in particular, with a new birth. Allahu Akbar! (God is Greator). He has blessed us with a leader in Imam W. Deen Muhammad, who does not fear anyone or anything but Allah! He is not moved by the "winds of emotion", and protects that that is whipped up by the Jahcubite conspirators. He is not bogged down with any identity crisis. Allah has blessed us with independent thinking leadership, and those of us who truly follow his leadership which is grounded in the Holy Qur'an and the Sunnah of Prophet Muhammad (PBUH), should never allow our minds to become shackled again!

Just as there were forces in the time of the Prophet that tried to crush out the light of Al-Islam, and just as there were forces that threatened the spread of truth by all the Prophets, there are forces in America and throughout the world that are trying to stop the spread of Al-Islam in the world, particularly among the ex-slaves of America. We are blessed! Allah has favored us! Allah has saved and restored us to our proper identity. We are Muslims of African decent, who live in America, not Arabia, Pakistan, Morroco, or Egypt! Our religion (Al-Islam) unites us with Muslims all over the world. Allah says in Al-Quran that **"He has made us different communities so that we may know one another, not despise one another"**. We must combat all negative images of Al-Islam.

Our religion is not a one-sided religion. It is not only concerned with the physical demands of life or only the spiritual side of life, but it addresses and develops both aspects of human life and society. Therefore, we, as Muslims, have an obligation to involve ourselves in every aspect of human development and societal development. We must get involved in the economic, political, social, educational, and spiritual activities of America and the world. Our involvement, however, must be based on the profound teachings of the Holy Qur'an and the Sunnah of the Prophet. Imam W. Deen Muhammad is constantly addressing and providing solutions to the many ills that plague our people and the world.

Those of us who say we accept Imam W. Deen Muhammad as our teacher must stand up like firm pillars and support him and his ideas and programs, not only with our words but with our hands (actions). This community has been divinely created and protected by Allah. The same Power that brought the sun, moon, and stars into existence, is the same power that brought this community under the leadership of Imam W. Deen Muhammad into existence. What does this mean? It means that there is no power on earth or in heaven that can destroy our community. There is no man or group of men that can destroy this community without the permission of Allah. Therefore all of the plots and schemes to destroy, misrepresent, misdirect this community through infiltration and other means, will meet with accumulated failure. Allahu Akbar!

"Oh Allah, Make Prophet Muhammad successful, and the followers of Muhammad successful, as Thou did make Abraham successful and the followers of Abraham successful. Oh Allah, Bless Muhammad, and the true followers of Muhammad, as Thou did Bless Abraham and the true followers of Abraham, for surely thou are praised and magnified."

FOOTNOTES

1. Holy Qur'an, 30:27, Yusuf Ali Translation

2. Ibid., 26:41-42

3. Imam W. Deen Muhammad, Prayer and Al-Islam, Muhammad Islamic Foundation, Chicago Illinois, 1982, p.16.

4. Holy Qur'an, 2:132

5. Ibid., 23:51-52

6. Hammudah Abdalati, Islam In Focus

7. W. D. Muhammad, The Teachings of W. D. Muhammad Book I, The Hon. Elijah Muhammad Mosque No. 2, 1976, p. 162

8. Muhammad Shamim Raza, M.A., D.J., Introducing The Prophets, S. H. Muhammad Ashraf, Lahore Pakistan 1969, p. 32

9. Muhammad Husayn Haykal, The Life of Muhammad, North America Trust Publications, 1976, p. 23

10. W. D. Muhammad, opt. cit., p. 93

11. Ibid., p. 31

12. Lecture - Truth That Lights the World

13. Holy Qur'an 27:103

14. W. D. Muhammad, Prayer and Al-Islam, op. cit., p. 154-55

15. Dr. M. Hafez Syed, Thus Spoke Prophet Muhammad, 1977, p. 48

16. Haykal, op. cit. p. 16

17. Abul Ala Maududi, The Prophet of Islam, Markazi Maktaba Jamaat-E-Islamic Hind, 1971, p. 2-3

18. W. D. Muhammad, Prayer and Al-Islam op. cit. p. 7

19. Afzal Ur Rahman, Muhammad Encyclopedia of Seerah, Vol. I, The Muslim Schools Trust, London, 1981 p. 22

20. Fakir Syed Waheed-Ud-Din The Benefactor, p. 61

21. W. D. Muhammad, Prayer and Al-Islam, op. cit. p. 52

22. Ibid., p. 12

23. Ibid., p. 16

24. J.A. Rogers, World's Great Men of Color, MacMillan Publishing CO., Inc., 1972, p. 133

25. Ibid., p. 150

26. Ibid., p. 175

27. Ibid., p. 238

28. Edward Blyden, Christianity, Islam, and the Negro Race, W. B. Whittingham, London, 1888, p. 256-266

29. J. A. Rogers, opt. cit., p. 19

30. Ibid., p. 14

31. Ibid., p. 118

32. W. D. Muhammad, Prayer and Al-Islam, opt. cit. p. 29

CHRISTIANITY

CHRISTIANITY

"Strongest among men in enmity to the Believers wilt thou find the Jews and the Pagans; And nearest among them in love to the Believers wilt thou find those who say "We are Christians": Because amongst these are men devoted to learning and men who have renounced the world, and they are not arrogant."
H.Q. 5:85

During the early part of the history of Prophet Muhammad (PBUH), we learned that many of the sincere and faithful followers of Jesus from Abyssinia respected the Muslim virtues and treated them with love and hospitality. Even today there are many truthful God-loving Christians who love Jesus Christ. If one looks at Christianity objectively, sincerely and rationally, he would have to admit that among other things, Christianity teaches good moral virtues and principles. If we compare briefly some of the moral teachings of Christianity and Al-Islam, we can see, and perhaps, understand and appreciate some of the similarities that exist.

Forgiveness

Christianity:

Peter said unto him, "Lord, how oft shall my brother sin against me, and I forgive him? Til seven times?" Jesus saith unto him, "I say not unto thee, until seven times: but, until seventy times seven." (Matthew 18:21-22)

-57-

Al-Islam:

"Quite a number of the People of the Book (i.e. followers of the other revealed religions) wish that they could turn you people back to infidelity after ye have believed, from selfish envy, after the truth hath become manifest unto them: But forgive and overlook till Allah accomplish His purpose: for Allah hath power over all things." (2:109)

Love and Sympathy

Christianity:

"Thou shalt love thy neighbor as thyself"

Al-Islam:

"No man is a true believer unless he desires for his brother that which he desires for himself." (Sayings of Muhammad)

Peace

Al-Islam:

"And the servants of the Beneficent God are they who walk on the earth in humility, and when the ignorant address them, they say, Peace" (25:63)

"A Muslim is he from whose tongue and hands people are safe, and a Muhajir is he who forsakes what God has forbidden." (Saying of Muhammad)

Christianity:

> "Blessed are the peacemakers: for they shall be called the children of God." (Matthew 5:9)

> "Behold, I send you forth as sheep in the midst of wolves; be ye therefore wise as serpents, and harmless as doves." (Matthew 5:5)

Politeness

Christianity:

> "But I say unto you, that whosoever is angry with his brother without a cause shall be in danger of judgment; and whosoever shall say to his brother, "Raca", shall be in danger of the Council: but whosoever shall say, "Thou fool", shall be in danger of hell fire." (Matthew 5:22)

Al-Islam:

> "O ye who believe!, let not some men among you laugh at others: it may be that the latter are better than the former. Nor let some women laugh at others; it may be that the latter are better than the former. Nor defame, nor be sarcastic to each other, nor call each other by offensive nicknames." (49:11-12)

> "And be moderate in thy pace and lower thy voice: for the harshest of sounds without doubt is the braying of the ass." (31:18-19)

Chastity

Christianity:

> "Ye have heard that it was said by them of old time, 'Thou shalt not commit adultery'; but I say unto you, That whosoever looketh on a woman to lust after her hath committed adultery with her already in heart." (Matthew 5:27-28)

Al-Islam:

> "Come not nigh to shameful deeds, whether open or secret." (6:151)

> "Nor come nigh to adultery: For it is a shameful (deed) and an evil, opening the road (to other evils)." (17:32)

Honesty

Al-Islam:

> "And in no wise covet those things in which Allah hath bestowed his gifts more freely on some of you than on others: to men is allotted what they earn, and to women what they earn." (4:32)

Christianity:

> "Thou shalt not covet they neighbor's house, thou shalt not covet thy neighbor's wife, nor his manservant, nor his maidservants, nor his ox, nor his ass, nor anything that is thy neighbor's." (Exodus 20:17)

Before going any further, I would like to address some questions to my Christian readers:

Do you agree that God the Creator of the heavens and the earth does not belong to any particular race, creed, color or nationality?

Do you agree that God is not black, white, red, yellow or brown?

If you agree to both these questions, then ask yourself, isn't it odd that the pictures of Jesus, the angels, and the saints are white? Perhaps right in your own home there is a picture of a Caucasian on your wall. More than likely, the Bible that you read and the Sunday school books that your children read have white images and pictures of Jesus, his disciples, the angels, etc. Why is that?

"What would happen if we (so-called Black people) were to try to get so-called white people to hang a picture of a black man on the walls of their churches and their homes and tell their people he is the Son of God and God?"

Consider this, what if someone broke into your home while you were there, robbed you of your belongings, murdered one of your family members and did all kinds of savage and shameful things to you. When he leaves he takes your daughter, or son, or mother, or wife hostage. What would you do? Would you get a picture of him (the criminal) and hang on your walls and worship him as God or the Son of God? You say, of course not!

Well, this is what happens to African-Americans. The Caucasian has been the criminal and we are the victims. This is not to say that you should not recognize any good contribution made by Caucasians, but it does mean that you should take down that Caucasian image of Jesus and know that we have been manipulated and conditioned through slavery to fear and worship them as God.

Should there be a black image of God? No! All images that attempt to portray the Almighty Creator should be removed!

A wise king named Solomon once said, **"Wisdom is the principal thing; therefore, get wisdom: and with all thy getting get undersanding."** It is a shame and disgrace that the pure teachings of Jesus Christ have been distorted and misrepresented throughout America and most of the world. It is vitally important for every sincere follower of Jesus to beware of the fact that many lies have been told on Christ Jesus and false claims made on his teachings. Know that his true message and life have been shrouded in mystery and symbolism. The **truth** that Jesus taught was crucified and buried. Therefore, it is not enough for the sincere Christian to just read the Bible and go to church on Sunday to hear the preacher. Jesus said, **"The kingdom of God is within."** (Luke 17:20-21). Truth and knowledge builds the temple.

If the sincere and faithful Christian (who has been classified as sheep) would dare to research the history of the church and its doctrine as it is preached today, he would be shocked by his findings. The history of the church is written in blood and paganism. The good Christians are not the architects and designers of Christianity, particularly African-American Christians who were just allowed in the church a little over a hundred years ago. In discussing attempts at writing the history of Christianity, one Alvin Boyd Kuhn states in his book, <u>Shadow of the Third Century: A Re-evaluation of Christianity</u>:

> Every attempt to write Christian history hitherto has been doomed to miscarriage from the start by its being based on presuppositions and acceptances not a single one of which could be certified as veridical truth, but all of which in the total amounted to a nearly complete tangle of falsehood. It has been constructed and still rests on an insecure and untenable platform of fiction, fantasy and falsity.....Perhaps no other religion has ever come so near to being based wholly on fiction, fancy and lurid imagination. (p. 7, 9).

Modern Christianity is a concoction of the infidels, disbelievers and pagans. It is not the religion of Jesus. He never knew of such doctrine. Jesus taught that God was one God not a trine God. The Bible tells us that the message of truth would be concealed from the world.

In the Book of Amos, (4:11-12), it reads,

"Behold, the day come, saith the Lord God, that I will send a famine in the land, not a famine of bread, nor of thirst for water, but of hearing the words of the Lord: And they shall wander from sea to sea, and from the north even to the east; they shall run to and fro to seek the word of the Lord, and shall not find it."

Jesus said, **"It is written, man shall not live by bread alone, but by every word that proceedeth out of the mouth of God."** (Matthew 4:4). If the word of God was to be concealed or lost from the people, as Amos states, then the life which the word gives would also be absent from among the people, thereby leaving them dead to truth and understanding. Jesus also said, **"I am the light of the world as long as I am in the world"** (John 9:5). The Bible (New Testament) was written and compiled after Jesus left this world, therefore, based on his own statement, it can be reasoned that the Bible was compiled during a time of darkness (ignorance and corruption).

Jesus also asked his disciples, "Why thou seek the living amongst the dead?" The deceivers of this world have conditioned us to such an extent that when the name Jesus is mentioned, the image of a paled faced Caucasian on a cross bleeding, instantly flashes into our minds.

According to the Christian doctrine, the twelve disciples of Jesus were Andrew, Bartholomew, James (son of Zebedee), James (Son of Alphacus), John, Judas Iscariot, Matthew, Peter, Philip, Simon, Thaddeus and Thomas. Of these twelve, two (John and Matthew) along with Luke and Mark (who were not disciples of Jesus) are credited for writing the "Gospel of Jesus." There is considerable suspicion about the authenticity of the Gospels, especially those of Luke and Mark. The Gospel or New Testament was not written until some fifty years after Jesus' death. It was not written while Jesus was alive. Jesus was not around to confirm or deny anything that was being said and written about him. Jesus never brought any "New Testament." Approximately four hundred years elapsed between the writing of Malachi, the last book of the Old Testament, and the beginning of the New Testament era.

"These Old Testament Scriptures were extensively used by Christ and His followers, and for more than a quarter of a century after Christ began his public ministry, they constituted the only written Bible of Christianity. For more than twenty-five years after Christ's ascension to heaven, the facts about his conception, birth, life and ministry, and the tenents of the Christian faith as taught by Jesus himself were propagated only by word of mouth."

The New Testament consists of twenty-seven books. It is basically a collection of four incomplete narrations of Jesus' earthly life and mission by four individuals (St. Matthew, St. Mark, St. Luke and St. John); the Acts of the "Apostles"; some Epistles (letters) most of them by St. Paul who never saw Jesus; and last, the Revelations of John.

The four Gospels included in the Bible are not the only Gospels that were written and accepted by many of the followers and believers of Jesus. There were several Gospels written during the early Christian era. (Some reports say there were as many as 300).

Huber L. Drumwright, Ph.D., in his "Introducing the Bible" writes: "A number of Christian writings other than those that came to be accepted for the New Testament appeared early and were considered by some to be worthy of canonical status. First and Second Clement, the Didache and Epistle of Barnabas, the Shepherd of Hermas, the Apocalypse of Peter, and the Acts of Paul were some of the more popular ones. By the beginning of the third century, twenty-two of the writings of our present New Testament had been widely accepted."[1] What happened to these other writings? Why were not they included in the present "New Testament"? It is because they gave a more accurate and truthful account of the life and teaching of Jesus Christ, the son of Mary. For example, Mark's grandfather, St. Barnabas, a close friend and apostle of Jesus, "selected by the Holy Spirit", in his writings, gives a more extensive report on Jesus' life. The Gospel of St. Barnabas was accepted and read in the churches until it was condemned in 496 of the Christian era by the Galatian Decree. Prior to it being condemned by the Galatian Decree, it was also condemned by Pope Damasus (303-384 A.D.) in 366 A.D.

Muhammad Ata Ur-Rahim points out that, "The Gospel of Barnabas is the only known surviving Gospel written by a disciple of Jesus, that is, by a man who spent most of his time in the actual company of Jesus during the three years in which he was delivering his message. He therefore had direct experience and knowledge of Jesus' teachings, unlike all the authors of the four accepted Gospels."[2] History reveals that this Gospel of Barnabas was also accepted in the churches of Alexandria up until 325 A.D. when the famous Council of Nicea was held. It was at this Council that the doctrine of the Trinity was born and declared to be the official doctrine of the Church. As a consequence of this decision, the other Gospels, most of which credited Jesus for teaching the concept of one God, was ordered to be completely destroyed. It was also decided that all Gospels written in Hebrew should be destroyed. All of the Gospels that contradicted the doctrine of Trinity were to be destroyed. Anyone found in possession of any of the unauthorized Gospels, after the decree had been made public, would be put to death.

The Gospels of Barnabas, however, were not totally destroyed. In fact, although they were forbidden to the general masses of people, they were still being referred to by the leaders of the Church. In fact, according to several reports, the Pope secured a copy of the Gospel of Barnabas in 383 A.D. and kept it in his private library. The Gospel of Barnabas is a very important document because it revealed among other things, that Jesus said that Muhammad would come after him. Muhammad is the Comforter that Jesus prophesied would come after him to bring the people into all truth. According to the Gospel of Barnabas, Jesus said to his disciples:

> **"I therefore say unto you that the messenger of God is a splendour that shall give gladness to nearly all that God hath made...And when I saw him, my soul was filled with consolation saying, 'O Muhammad, God be with thee, and may he make me worthy to untie thy shoelatchet, for obtaining this I shall be a great prophet and holy one of God."**[3]

The four Gospels that appear in the New Testament do not claim to be divinely inspired, nor were they regarded as such by the early Christians. What was divinely inspired was the teachings of Jesus himself. It is generally accepted by many of the Christian scholars and researchers that the Gospels were influenced by other sources. One such source is known as "Q" or "Quelle" (German for "Source"), a lost Aramaic document. Matthew and Luke, it is believed, incorporated this document into their Gospels. Another early document known as "L" is a collection of reports about Jesus used only by Luke. Then there is another called "Urmacus" which is supposed to be an early draft of Mark's Gospel, written on the basis of Peter's discourses. It is sometimes referred to as the Triple Tradition because it was also used by the writers of the Gospels according to Luke and Matthew. Dr. Huber L. Drumwright writes, "Matthew, Mark and Luke are called the "Synoptic Gospels" because they are so closely related and share a common point of view. John's Gospel in many ways preserve and independent tradition and is by far, the most interpretative of these books."[4]

As one inquistor asked, "Why did God reveal His word to these four writers and why did He not adopt the more reasonable course of revealing His word to the founder himself?" According to the Scriptures, the Creator revealed his message directly to His Prophet Moses (PBUH). Prophet Muhammad (PBUH) received the last revelation—the Holy Qur'an. Prophet Muhammad instructed his followers and companions to write the revelations down on their hearts and on sheets. Ulfat Aziz Us-Samad writes, "The revelations came down to him (Muhammad) in fragments, from time to time. As soon as he received one, he used to communicate it to his disciples and ask them to write them down. On each such occasion, he indicated in a precise manner the place to which the revelation belonged...Another step that the Holy Prophet took to save the Qur'an from the fate that had overtaken the earlier Scriptures, including the Gospel of Jesus, was to ask his followers to learn the Qur'an by heart...Thus the whole of the Qur'an was committed to writing and also preserved in the memories of hundreds of persons in the lifetime of the Holy Prophet."[5]

Dr. Maurice Bucaille, in his book The Bible, The Quran and Science, writes:

"Thanks to its undisputed authenticity, the text of the Qur'an holds a unique place among the Books of Revelation, shared neither by the Old nor the New Testament... In the case of the Old Testament, the sheer number of authors who tell the same story, plus all the revision carried out on the text of certain books from the pre-Christian era, constitute as many reasons for inaccuracy and contradiction. As for the Gospels, nobody can claim that they invariably contain faithful accounts of Jesus' words or a description of his actions strictly in keeping with reality...

The situation is very different for the Qur'an. As the Revelation progressed, the Prophet and the believers following him recited the text by heart and it was also written down by the scribes in his following. It therefore starts off with two elements of authenticity that the Gospels do not possess."[6]

The Creator tells us in the Qur'an that He has protected it from crookedness and error. It reads, **"Praise be to God, who hath sent His servant the Book, and hath allowed therein no crookedness."** (18:1)

The Bible was corrected and made pure in the Holy Qur'an. The Holy Qur'an confirms and corrects all the previous Scriptures. The Bible, particularly the New Testament that is used by Christians today, does not contain in its fullness the true word of God. There is some truth in the Bible but it is covered with symbolisms, parables and mysteries. There are many Christians who will agree with this fact. The Unitarians and the Essenes rebelled against the idea of the Trinity and many of them still believe in the oneness of God as it was properly taught by Prophet Jesus.

In concluding this section, I would like to make a few brief points: The reader should bear in mind that (1) the first Gospel to be written was the Gospel of St. Mark (70 C.E.) and it is actually an expanded version of Urmarcus (which is believed to have been his first manuscript); Mark's oldest manuscripts do not contain verses 9 to 20 of the last chapter of his present Gospel, dealing with the resurrection and ascension of Jesus. (The Life of Jesus by C.J. Cadoux, p. 13). (2) The Gospel of St. Matthew was written in Greek at Antioch around 90 C.E. (3) The Gospel of St. Luke was written in Greece about 1000 C.E. for the benefit of the "Most Excellent." It is generally viewed as an apologetic address to non-Jews. (4) The Gospel of John was written near Ephesus between the years 110 and 115 C.E. (Christian Era) by an unknown writer who was anti-semitically inclined.

In _A Comparative Study of Christianity and Islam_ which was conducted by Mrs. Us-Samad of the University of Peshawar (Pakistan), eleven important points pertaining to the history of Jesus and the Gospels were highlighted. She pointed out, based on her research that:

--No written copy was made of the inspired sayings of Jesus during his lifetime;

--The earliest records of Jesus, which were shortly after his death, have been completely and irretrievably lost.

--That in the Gospels, which were written between 70 and 115 C.E. on the basis of some of those documents, the material contained in them was handled very freely; the Evangelists felt no hesitation in altering it for what they considered to be the greater glory of Christ or to bring it in line with the view of their respective sects.

--The Evangelists very often put their own words into the mouth of Jesus;

--None of the Evangelists had known Jesus or heard him speaking;

--The Gospels were written in Greek, whereas the language spoken by Jesus was Aramaic;

--The (Gospels) were composed to propagate the points of view of the different factions and that they were chosen from many others that represented different viewpoints;

--For at least a century after they were written they had no canonical authority and so could be and were actually changed by copyists of the different sects to serve their own purposes;

--The earliest extant manuscripts of the Gospels belong to the fourth and fifth centuries, and no one knows how much the Gospels had been changed during the centuries of which no manuscript is available;

--That there are many differences at many places

among the various extant manuscripts of the fourth and fifth centuries;

--The gospels taken as a whole are full of contradictions.

During Jesus' lifetime, he was known as "Jesus of Nazareth" and his followers were called "Nazarenes". Saul of Tarus (who later changed his name to Paul), a converted Jew, was the key factor in introducing many new ideas in what was to be called "Christianity". History also reveals that the early disciples taught the Unitarian Concept of Christianity, the belief in the Oneness of God. It was Paul, however, who introduced the Three-in-One concept of God which was adopted by the Nicene Council in 325 A.D.

THE NICENE COUNCIL

The term and concept of the Trinity was adopted in the year 325 A.D. at a Religious Council held in the city of Nicea in the Roman province of Bithyania, a country in Asia Minor. The Council was convened at the request of Constantine, the Emperor of Rome. History tells us that 318 bishops were present at the convention and through an elected process, the divinity of Jesus was established. According to some reports, 313 of the 318 bishops present voted in favor of this falsehood.

Ata-ur-Rahim writes, "That this historic decision was based first as much on political expediency as on faulty reasoning of philosophy, is shown by the part played by Constantine, the pagan Emperor of Rome, who presided over Nicea. The growing communities of Christians were a force whose opposition he had no wish for, who weakened his Empire and whose support would be invaluable in strengthening it. By remodeling Christianity, he hoped to gain the Church's support and, at the same time, end the confusion which had arisen within it... which was the source of yet more conflict within his Empire." (Jesus, A Prophet of Islam).

This degeneration of the true teachings of Christ Jesus the son of Mary, which resulted in the acceptance of a three-god Christianity, never went unchallenged. When, in 325 A.D., the doctrine of Trinity was officially proposed as the orthodox Christian doctrine, Arius, a Christian leader in North Africa, stood up against the combined strength of Constantine and the Catholic Church and reminded them that Jesus had always affirmed the Divine Unity. According to history, Constantine used all the force and brutality at his command to try to crush those people who believed in the One God, but he failed. Nevertheless, the doctrine of the Trinity was eventually accepted as the official basis of Christianity in Europe.

Ata-ur-Rahim also observed, "The Church made religion

not only independent of the Scriptures, but also independent of Jesus, so that the man Jesus became confused with a mythological Christ. Belief in Jesus, however, does not necessarily mean belief in a resurrected Christ. Whereas the immediate followers of Jesus had based their lives on his example, Pauline Christianity was based on a belief in Christ after his supposed crucifixion, and the life and teachings of Jesus while he was alive was no longer important."[7]

We further find that in the 4th century, when Christianity became the state religion, following the conversion of the Roman Emperor Constantine, the doctrine of the diety of Jesus as expounded by Catholics was officially established. All other views were suppressed by "fire and sword." It was, indeed, the Nicene Creed that declared that Jesus was God of God, Light of Lights, King of Kings and Lord of Lords--not Jesus Christ, the Prophet (Peace be upon Him). The Holy Qur'an says, **"They do blaspheme who say: 'God is Christ the son of Mary'; But said Christ: 'O Children of Israel! Worship God, my Lord and your Lord (5:75). "Christ the son of Mary was no more than an apostle; many were the apostles that passed away before him." (5:78).**

CONSTANTINE THE EMPEROR

Under the reign and auspices of Constantine, Christianity as we know it today, became an established religion. Constantine was born on the 27th of February in the year of Christ 272. His father's name was Flavius Valerius Constantuis, surnamed Chlorus; and his mother's name was Helena. When Constantine came into power in Rome, there was great conflict between the various Christian and pagan religious sects in Rome. By the end of the year 324 A.D., the conflict and confusion had become so intense and dangerous that something had to be done before the whole Roman Empire became engulfed in internal strife. The greatest conflict was between the Pauline and Apostolic Churches. Constantine saw this as an opportunity to escalate his authority. According to history, Constantine went to all kinds of extremes to insure that he became the Emperor

-72-

of Rome. To make sure of his position as Emperor, he even had his own son, Crispus, murdered. We learn from history that Constantine became jealous of his eldest son who had become very popular in Rome. It appeared that he (Crispus) was destined to unseat his father. It was also known, however, that Crispus' stepmother wanted her own son to succeed Constantine. It is believed that she therefore, had intentions of murdering Crispus. Constantine, however, beat her to the punch, and blamed the murder on the stepmother. He then killed her by immersing her in a tub of boiling water. These vicious acts of murder did not go unchallenged. The supporters of the dead queen joined forces with the followers of his son Crispus, and both sought revenge.

It became so uncomfortable for Constantine, that he decided to go to Byzantium. Upon arriving there, he renamed the city after himself and called it Constantinople. It was here where he received "unexpected" success from the Pauline Church. Ata-Ur-Rahim explains that,

> "They said that if he (Constantine) did penance in their church, his sins would be forgiven. Constantine made full use of this facility... Having salved his conscience with his confession, the life to come ceased to worry him and he turned his attention to the affairs of the Empire. He saw the possibilities of using the church to his own ends provided that he could win its loyalty to him, so he gave the church his full support."[8]

While traveling with his soldiers Constantine had a dream which inspired him to launch his diabolical scheme. It is reported that in his dream he saw in the sky a pillar of light in the form of a cross whereon was engraved the inscription, "In this overcome". The following night, he had another dream in which he claims Jesus appeared before him saying, "Frame to thyself the form of a cross after the example of the sign which appeared unto thee, and bear the same against thy enemies as a fit banner, a token of victory." With the backing of Constantine, the Church became an established force almost overnight. He used the Church to conquer his enemies. Many of the priests were used to carry out very useful intelligence work for him and their help was also an important factor in his attempts at uniting Europe and the Middle East under him.

The sincere and truthful Christians of today would find it very beneficial and enlightening to do some research on Constantine and the history of the Church. Perhaps you will learn that Constantine (who is referred to by some Christian authorities as "The Beloved of God") was a true pagan and murderer. This man drowned his own wife, Fausta, beheaded his eldest son, Crispus (in the same year that he presided over the Nicean Council), he murdered his own father-in-law, Maximian Herculius, he murdered both his sisters' husbands, he also murdered his nephew, the son of his sister Constantia. This child was only twelve years old. Reverend Robert Taylor explains in his book The Diegesis that these murders happened very near to one another when Constantine had reached the peak of his fortune and was in the "greatest prosperity". Taylor writes,

> "Reader! imagine thou seest his noble son imploring a father's mercy--but in vain. Imagine thou seest his innocent wife supplicating for rather any other death at his hands that than most horrible one of the boiling bath--but in vain. Think that thou seest the poor unoffending child upon his knees, lifting his innocent hands to beg his life, and his most "holy" uncle will not regard him. think that thou hearest the distracted shrieks of the fond doating mother, the beautiful Constantia with dishevelled hair and heart-broken moans, entreating her brother to spare her, but in vain.

Not a wife's anguish nor a sister's tears, nor nearest of kindred, nor matchless woman's tenderness, nor guileless youth's innocence could soften the heart of this evangelical cut-throat, this "godly" and "holy" child-killer." (p.349).

Yet, this man Constantine, is lauded as a "great saint' of Christianity. In fact, Lardner states, "Constantine the Emperor, fixing his whole mind upon such things as set forth the glory of God, behaved himself in all things as becometh a Christian, erecting chruches from the ground, and adorning them with godly and gorgeous consecrated ornaments." J.D. Buck informs us that, "This same Constantine who, with his soldiers, environed the Bishops at the first Council of Nice, A.D. 325, and dictated terms of the deliberations, applied for initiation into the Mysteries, and was told by the officiating priest that no purgation could free him from the crime of putting his wife to death, or from his many perjuries and murders." (Mystery Masonry, p. 53)

Constantine being a pagan worshipper himself, introduced and incorporated many of the pagan ideas and customs into the teaching of the church.

MYTHOLOGICAL AND PAGAN INFLUENCE

According to Imam Alauddin Shabazz, Constantine "was the first universal bishop of Christianity even though he was all but completely ignorant of Jesus' teachings. He was a follower of the solar cult of Mittras (the Iranian God of Light)... What happened at the supra council? The dogma of the trinity of father, son and holy ghost was introduced into Christianity... It was done by a coterie of pastors known by theological experts as the "Rump Council"... Today, the church still feeds, mentally, on the dogma of the trinity that was added to the other falsification found in Christianity."[10]

Christianity, as understood and believed by most Christians today, is based on five fundamental doctrines of belief: (1) The Trinity; (2) The Divinity of Jesus; (3) The Divine Sonship of Jesus; (4) The Original Sin,; and (5) The Atonement. Jesus Christ, the son of Mary, never taught these doctrines of belief. Let us look briefly at each of these ideas.

The Trinity holds that there are three separate and distinct Divine Beings in the Godhead, i.e. Father, Son and Holy Ghost. According to the Bible (Mark 12:29-30) Jesus taught that God was One, having no partners. In Matthew (6:10) it is reported that Jesus said, **"Thou shalt worship the Lord thy God and him only shalt thou serve."** Allah (God) tells us in the Holy Qur'an that **"He is One God, the Eternal, Absolute; He begetteth not nor is He begotten: and there is none like unto Him** (Chapter 112). The Qur'an also says, **"So believe in Allah and His messengers, and say not three—cease! (it is) better for you! Allah is only One God."** (4:171).

The second belief, the divinity of Jesus, is generally based on the idea that Jesus was born of a virgin mother, without the agency of a man. If that is the case, then Melchisedec and Adam should be considered divine also. The Bible says that Melchisedec was a king of peace and righteousness and was born of neither father or mother; he had neither beginning of days, nor end of life (Hebrews 7:1-3). Adam was also created without mother or father, but from the dust of the earth. The Holy Qur'an says that, **"...the similitude of Jesus before God is as that of Adam; He created him from dust, then said to him 'Be' and he was,"** (3:59). It also says that **"Jesus and his mother is a sign".** Jesus wrestled with those who wanted to make a diety of him. We read (in Mark 10:17-18) that Jesus was addressed as "Good Master" and responded **"Why callest thou me good? There is none good but One, that is God."**

The next belief, which claims that Jesus is the son of God, could not be farther from the truth. This idea, although it appears in the New Testament, requires some interpretation. A son of God can be understood to mean a follower of God's way, one who submits his will to do the will of God. Jesus was born during a time of great sin and corruption. Only God could give spiritual birth to a man during a time of spiritual darkness. According to the Bible, Jesus said, **"we all are the children of the Most High God."** In John (20:27) Jesus spoke of God as **"My Father and your Father, and my God and your God."** He made no distinction between his relation to God and any other human beings' relationship to God. Furthermore, the title "Son of God" is used in the Bible referring to Israel (Exdous 4:22), David (Psalms 2:7) and Solomon (1 Chronicles 22:10). Therefore, if Jesus ever used the expression "Son of God" for himself as the New Testament says, it was no doubt in the same sense in which it was applied to Israel, David and Solomon. The Qur'an clears up the confusion. It says, **"They say: 'God hath begotten a son': Glory be to Him (God)—Nay, to Him belongs all that is in the heavens and on earth: everything renders worship to Him"** (2:116). **"No son did God beget nor is there any god along with Him"** (23:91). **"To Him (God) is due the primal origin of the heavens and the earth: How can He have a son when He hath no consort?"** (6:101).

Actually, the idea of Son of God is a corruption of the term "Sun" god. During the time of Jesus and many years before and after him, there existed many pagan cults that worshipped the sun and its influences (i.e. generative powers). In ancient times, the sun was used as a symbol of God because it provided light, warmth, growth, etc.

The fourth fundamental belief, original sin, holds that each human being is born in sin because Adam disobeyed the Creator by eating from the forbidden tree. (Gen. 2:16-17). In the Book of Romans (5:12) it reads, **"By one man sin entered into the world, and death by sin; and so death passed upon all men, for that all have sinned."** According to this belief, man's nature is sinful, each child is born a sinner because of Adam's transgression about 6,000 years ago. This particular belief is the premise on which the fifth belief—the Atonement (crucifixion of Jesus) is based. In other words, if Adam did not sin then there would not have been a need for Jesus to come and give his life **"for the sins of the world"** according to Christianity.

It is ironic that Christianity claims that every man, woman and child was/is born in sin from the time of Adam, and that only through Jesus can man's sins be forgiven. Yet the Bible tells us that God saved many righteous prophets from amongst human beings. Abraham, Moses, Job, Jacob, Solomon, and many others that came before Jesus were blessed and favored by God (according to Christianity). Abraham was born thousands of years before Jesus, yet the Bible gives us a picture of him in heaven (Luke 16:22-13). Elijah, the Bible says, **was taken up to heaven full body and soul.** The fact is that Jesus nor the other prophets ever taught that one man could inherit the sins of another. They taught that every man was responsible and accountable for his own actions, and that children would not be punished for the sins of their fathers. In the Book of Ezekiel, it reads, **"The son shall not bear the iniquity of the father, neither shall the father bear the iniquity of the son: the righteousness of the righteous shall be upon him, and the wickedness of the wicked shall be upon him."** (18:20). Jeremiah the Prophet also said, **"In those days they shall say no more, the father have eaten a sour grape, and the children's teeth are set on edge. But every one shall die for his own iniquity; every man that eateth the sour grape, his teeth shall be set on edge."** (31:29-30). In the Psalms, it reads **"Lo, children are an heritage of the Lord: and the fruit of the womb is his reward."** (127:3) According to Mark, Jesus said, **"Suffer the little children to come unto me, and forbid them not, for of such is the Kingdom of God."** (10:14-15).

In Al-Islam, the human being is placed on a plane of dignity. The Qur'an says that **man was created in the best mould** (95:4). Man does not start life in sin with a perverted nature. Why would God be so cruel, unjust and merciless? As one author writes, "It is the height of misanthropy and cynicism to consider children to be sinful at birth." God is the All-Forgiving, All-Merciful. Allah (God) tells us in the Holy Qur'an that, **"If any one doeth evil or wrongs his own soul, but afterwards seeks God's forgiveness, he will** find God oft-forgiving, Most Merciful. And if any one earns sin, he earns it against his own soul: for God is full of knowledge and wisdom" (4:110-111).

This brings us now to the fifth belief---"**the Atonement**". <u>This idea claims that Jesus was born for the sole purpose of dying for the sins of mankind.</u> He is referred to as the "Second Adam." We should ask ourselves if Jesus came to redeem man by sacrificing his life, why did he wait until he was thirty three years old and why did he pray "**Father, all things are possible unto Thee; take away this cup from me.**" (Mark 14:36).

Reader, ask yourself, has sin decreased in the world since the time of Jesus or has it increased? Has not sin increased? Then what good was this so-called blood sacrifice? It never happened, and to suggest that it did, especially for the reasons generally given, is an insult and blasphemy of the Creator. The Bible presents God as a failure. First He tries to make a righteous man but fails; the man Adam disobeyed. Then He raises a prophet named Lot, but he sleeps with his daughter. Noah gets drunk; David conspired to have his general killed so he can get Sheba, his general's wife. Then He causes Mary to have an unnatural birth so that Jesus could be murdered in hopes that man would cease his sinful ways, but that failed.

In the Book of Hebrews (5:7) it tells us that Jesus was afraid to die, he did not want to give up his precious life. Jesus was concerned about bringing the people out of darkness into the light, with the pure message of truth. He said, "**the truth will set you free.**" God is not concerned with blood sacrifice. The Qur'an says, "**It is not their meat nor their blood that reaches God: it is your piety that reaches Him.**"

According to history there were several mystery cults in Rome during the formation of the Christian doctrine. We find that each of them had at least four characteristics in common: (1) Each believed in a saviour-god, whose death was an atonement of the sins of man and a way to salvation

for those who believed. (2) Each cult had an initiation ceremony through which its converts or initiates had to pass.
(3) Each believed in mystery communions with God and involved a symbolic eating of his flesh and drinking of his
blood. (4) Each one looked forward to the Hereafter and
secured for the initiate a happy reception in the next life.
These same ideas and practices are events in the Christian
idea of Baptism and Eucharist.

Baptism is an initiatory rite by which a man is cleansed
of the original sin, "transformed from the child of wrath
into the child of grace." In the latter (the Eucharist or the
Holy Communion) the participant is made to eat a dry cracker
and drink red wine, which is supposed to be symbolic of
eating the flesh and drinking the blood of Jesus Christ.
Some Christian demoninations believe that the cracker and
wine are actually converted into the flesh and blood of Jesus.
This is called the "transubstantiation." Lord Raglan, in
his book The Origin of Religion, traces the origin of the
mystery cults to what he regards one of the earliest rituals,
a sort of restoration rite. He points out that in prehistoric
times it was the custom in several communities to select
a young man as the "destined divine victim" and to keep
him with divine honours for a year. At the end of the year,
however, he was ritually slaughtered and his flesh was eaten
and blood drunk by certain men of the community to bring
new life to all those on whose behalf this rite was performed.
Portions of the flesh and blood of the sacrificed man were
also scattered over the field to give it fertility and revive
the world.

This idea of a saviour-god later became fused with
the myth of the sun-god, as a result each one of them is
said to have been born around the time of the Winter Solstice
(according to the old Julian calendar this occurred on December 25th). Additionally, each of the saviour sun gods were
violently killed, but returned to life at the time of the Vernal
Equinox (springtime). It is no accident that the birth of
Jesus, according to Christianity, took place on December
25th, nor is it a coincident that he was violently murdered
and resurrected during the spring.

THE CHRISTIAN/EGYPTIAN CONNECTION

Let us examine further the "pagan and mythical connection". There are very clear similarities between the story of Jesus and the various sun-god myths: Osiris, Isis and Horus of Egypt, Baal of the Northern Semites, Tammuz of the Babylonians, Hercules of Romans, Mirtha of the Persians, Dionysus of the Greeks, and Hiram Abiff of Jerusalem (according to Freemasonry).

The Masons and Shriners, of which many are Christian preachers, trace the history and the idea of the trinity back to Ancient Egypt; and they understand the connection between the Christian belief in the birth, death resurrection, and the trinity as with that of the Egyptian Osirian mystery.

In looking at the idea of the saviour-god, we find that it was believed that nearly all of them were: (1) born around December 25th, (2) they were born of virgin mothers, (3) their father was a king or great man, (4) the father was always a near relative of the mother, but (5) the circumstances of their conception were unnatural, (6) they are called by the names Light Bringer, Healer, Son of God, Savior or Deliverer, (7) at their birth an attempt is usually made to kill them, (8) they usually escape the murderers' plot by being spirited away to a secret hiding place, (9) they are raised by foster parents in a far country (10) very little is revealed about their childhood, (11) on reaching manhood they usually return to public life, (12) they usually defeat the enemy or forces of darkness in their first battle, (13) they become a king, (14) they prescribe laws, (15) later they lose favor with the gods and/or their subordinates, then (16) they are cast down from the throne and driven out of the city, after which (17) they are murdered on top of a hill, (18) their children, if any, do not succeed them, (19) their body is not buried but placed in a sacred place, (20) the, rise again from the dead and become "pioneers of mankind to the heavenly world". Let us reflect and compare the story of Jesus.

According to the Christian story of Jesus, (1) his mother was a virgin, and (2) his father Joseph was a descendant of Prophet David, the King. (3) Joseph was closely related to Mary, (4) Jesus was conceived not by man, but by the Holy Ghost, (5) He is called the Savior, the Light of the World, the Son of Man, and the Son of God (6) Shortly after his brith, Herod the King makes an attempt to kill him, (7) Jesus escapes by being taken away to an isolated place, (8) He is raised by Mary and his foster father, Joseph, in the distant county of Egypt, (9) Gospels reveal very little about his childhood, (10) He returns when he reaches the age of twelve and begins preaching publicly, (11) Before he begins his public ministry, he had overcome Satan, (12) He is crucified along with two thieves, (13) His place of crucifixion was on top a hill called Calvary Golgotha, (14) As a result there is now in Jerusalem a holy sepulchre where Christians go to pay homage to Christ Jesus.

In analyzing the Egyptian myth of Osiris, the Christian story of Jesus and the Masonic story of Hiram Abiff, we find some convincing proofs that they actually refer to the same ideas and principles, and that Christianity as we know it today has adapted and incorporated many pagan customs and mythological ideas. Winwood Reade writes, "Christianity had conquered paganism and paganism had corrupted Christianity. The legends which belonged to Osiris and Apollo had been applied to the life of Jesus."

According to the noted Masonic author Edmond Ronayne, "Every part of freemasonry emphatically proclaims its pagan origin and that the god of its worship and religious philosophy is the old sun-god of the 'Ancient Mysteries'—the Osiris of the Egyptians or the Boal of the idolatrous Israelites". (The Master's Carpet, p. 331). Here we will attempt to establish the connection between the Legend of Hiram Abiff, the Widow's Son, and the myth of the Osiris; then we will draw a parallel between the story of Hiram Abiff and the story of Jesus. In the Traditions of Freemasonry, p. 240, it reads, "We readily recognize in Hiram Abiff the Osiris of the Egyptians, the Mithras of the Persians, the Bacchus of the Greeks."

HIRAM ABIFF, THE MASTER BUILDER

According to the tradition of Freemasonry, Hiram Abiff was the Chief Architect and Grand Master Builder of Solomon's Temple. According to the legend, King Solomon, Hiram King of Tyre, and Hiram Abiff made an agreement never to reveal the "Master's Word" until the Temple was complete, and only when all three of them were present. One day a misfortune fell upon Hiram Abiff while he was on his way to his working quarters to offer up his devotion to God and draw his designs on the trestle board. Masonic legend tells us that there was a conspiracy and plot hatched by fifteen "Fellow Crafts" to either extort the Master's Word from Hiram Abiff or kill him. However, after deep reflection and due consideration of the seriousness of such a crime, twelve of them reneged, but the other three, Jubela, Jubelo and Jubelum continued in their murderous scheme.

The ritual states that these three ruffians "placed themselves at the South, West and East gates of the inner court of the Temple and there awaited his return." The first ruffian, Jubela, approached him from the south of the Temple and requested the Word, but Hiram refused. In a rage, Jubela struck him across the throat with the twenty-four inch gauge. In an attempt to escape, Hiram ran towards the West, only to be met by the second ruffian, Jubelo, who also demanded the Master's Word. Hiram again refused to give him the Word, but Jubelo being more quick in his anger, swiftly struck him with the square across the left breast. Hiram then tried to make an escape through the East gate, where he is met by the third ruffian, Jubelum, who also demands of him the Master's Word. Again he refused to impart the Word. Jubelum, then explained in an angry tone, "Die then!" and struck him with the setting maul on the forehead which finally killed him. He was assaulted and murdered at twelve noon.

Then they buried him in the rubbish of the Temple until twelve midnight. Later they returned and moved the body in a westerly course and buried it in a shallow grave dug six feet perpendicular due East and West, on top of a hill west of Mount Moriah. An acacia was planted at the head of the grave to conceal it, "and that the place may be known should occasion thereafter ever require it." They then attempted to flee to Ethiopia, but was unable to because they did not have the "password."

According to the legend, King Solomon upon arriving at the Temple the next day and finding the labors in confusion, and no designes upon the trestle-board, became concerned about Hiram Abiff. Solomon was also informed that Hiram Abiff had not been seen since twelve noon the day before. Fearing his safety, Solomon ordered a strict search of every apartment of the Temple. Not finding him anywhere in the Temple, Solomon ordered the Grand Secretary to take roll-call, to see if any of the craft were missing along with Hiram Abiff. The roll-call revealed that Jubela, Jubelo and Jubelum were missing. The other twelve Fellow Crafts who were originally a part of the plot, but recanted, stepped forward and presented themselves before King Solomon, admitted their part in the plot and sought forgiveness. King Solomon ordered the twelve Fellow Crafts to divide themselves into parties and travel three East, three West, three North and three South in search of the murderers and "that which was lost."

The party that traveled a westerly course met a captain down near the port of Joppa and asked if he had seen any strangers pass that way. He informed them he had seen three, and described them as workmen from the Temple at Jerusalem seeking passage into Ethiopia, but not having King Solomon's pass, were unable to obtain a passage and returned back into the country. This party returned back to Solomon and communicated this information to him. It is reported that he instructed them to disguise themselves and travel as before, with positive injunctions to find the ruffians and with a positive assurance that if they did not, the twelve Fellow Crafts would be deemed guilty of the murder and severely suffer for the crime committed. They departed a second time in search of the body.

On returning, after several days of fruitless searching, one of them, being more weary than the others, sat down at the brow of a hill where Hiram was buried. On attempting to arise to his feet, he accidentally caught hold of an acacia, which easily giving way, excited his curiosity, whereupon he hailed his companions and on their examination found the appearance of a newly made grave. At that moment, Jubela's voice is heard, "Oh, that my throat had been cut across, my tongue torn out by its roots and buried in the rough sands of the sea at low water mark, where the tide ebbs and flows twice in twenty-four hours, ere I had consented to the death of so great a man as our Grand Master Hiram Abiff." Then, Jubelum exclaimed, "Oh, that my body had been cut in two, my bowels taken from thence and burned to ashes and the ashes scattered to the four winds of heaven, so that no more trace or remembrance might be had of so vile and perjured a wretch as I, ere I had caused the death of so great and so good a man as our Grand Master Hiram Abiff." Another voice was heard, "Ah, Jubela and Jubelo, it is I who am more guilty than you both; it was I who struck the fatal blow, it was I who killed him!" The three ruffians are captured and taken to Solomon, who upon due conviction and confession of their guilt, ordered them to be executed.

It is further explained, according to Freemasonry, that King Solomon then ordered the twelve Fellow Crafts to go in search of Hiram's body and when it is found to check for the Master's Word or a key to it. The body was found, and the only thing on it was the jewel of his office which was taken to Solomon. He then ordered the twelve Fellow Crafts to go and assist him in raising the body, and as the Master's Word was then lost, it was agreed between himself and Hiram, King of Tyre, that the first sign given on arriving at the grave, and the first word spoken after the body had been raised, would be adopted as the sign and substitute word for the regulation of all Master's lodges until future generations find the correct word. Upon approaching the grave and seeing their dead brother, the Master Builder, Hiram Abiff, Solomon and his Craftmen all threw their hands up and exclaimed, "Oh Lord, my God, was there no help for the widow's son? Oh Lord, my God, I fear that the Master's Word is forever lost!"

Solomon then ordered one of the Fellow Crafts to try and raise the dead body with the Entered Apprentice grip. Because the body had been dead for fifteen days, the skin slipped, making it unable to be raised. King Solomon then said to Hiram King of Tyre, "My worthy companion of Tyre, you will now take the body by the Fellow Craft's grip and see if it can be so raised." The skin slipped again. King Solomon then took the body by the strong grip of a Master Mason (also called the Lion's Paw) and raised it from a dead level to a living perpendicular to the square on the five points of Fellowship. The substitute word is "Mah-hah—bone."

Now we turn our attention to the Legend of Osiris, the ancient Egyptian sun-god. Observe very carefully the parables.

THE OSIRIAN MYTH

According to the legend, Osiris, as King of Egypt, applied himself to the civilizing of his nation, turning the Egyptians from their previously indigent and barbarous course of life to a happy community existence. It is reported that he taught them agriculture and established a code of conduct of ethics. He instructed them in the reverencing and worship of the gods, "thus establishing Egypt in all the essentials of truth." Osiris, after having established Egypt on a sound foundation, travelled over the rest of the world, "converting others to his disciplines, not by force but by persuasion of reason."

In the meantime, his brother, Typhon, was plotting to usurp the throne. Typhon persuaded seventy-two persons to join him in his conspiracy. He made a chest exactly to the measure of the body of Osiris and brought it with him to a banquet that was being held in Osiris' honor. During the entertainment, and while the guests were extolling the beauty of the chest, Typhon promised to give it to anyone whose body it would most conveniently fit. Each of the princes laid down in the chest but each was too tall or too short. Lastly, Osiris was tempted and convinced to try and see if it fitted him. Immediately after he laid down in the chest, the seventy-two conspirators rushed to the box, clamped the cover and nailed it shut and poured melted lead over all the cracks. The chest was then carried to the banks of the Nile and cast into the river.

When his sister-wife, Isis, was informed of the death of Osiris, she cut off one of the locks of her hair and put on the mourning apparel of widowhood. Immediately thereafter, "in the extremity of sorrow and despair at the loss of her husband" she set forth in search of Osiris' body. She wandered to and fro all throughout Egypt asking everyone with who she came in contact. Finally she is told by some young children that the chest or coffin had been carried by the waters out to sea and ended up in Bayblas, where it was lodged in the branches of a bush of the tamarind which had "grown up miraculously about the chest or coffin and concealed it within its trunk." It is reported that the King of Bayblas ordered the tree to be cut down, and from the trunk containing the coffin he made a pillar or column to support the roof of his palace.

According to the legend, Isis, by divine guidance, arrived in Bayblas and discovered the coffin. She then returned to Egypt (where her son, Horus, now reigned) and placed the body in a secret place. One night Typhon, while hunting, chanced upon the chest with Osiris' body in it. This time Typhon cut the body into fourteen pieces and scattered them throughout Egypt. When Isis found out what had happened, she undertook a second journey in search of each piece of Osiris' body. Each part of the body she found, she buried, separately. Finally, she recovered all of the parts of Osiris' body except his phallus which had been thrown into the river and eaten by three fish. Being unable to recover this organ, she made a substitute phallus of gold and performed a certain ceremony which enabled Osiris to be resurrected in the "underworld." After his resurrection, his spirit visits Isis and as a consequence she gives birth to another son, "as it were, by a Holy Ghost, for she knew no living man."

Now, let us compare more closely the similarities by looking at the principle details of both stories. In the Egyptian story of Osiris we find:

1) There is the possession of something valuable, Osiris possessed a kingdom.

2) There is a conspiracy—Typhon and his followers conspire against Osiris.

3) There is a conflict between Osiris and Typhon.

4) There is death—Osiris is murdered.

5) The death is by his brother.

6) The body is buried at the foot of a tamarind tree.

7) There is a first search by Isis.

8) She questions everyone she meets.

9) The search is accidentally successful.

10) There is a second search—Isis searches for the fourteen pieces of Osiris' body.

11) There is a finding—Isis finds all the parts of the body except one.

12) There is something forever lost—one part of Osiris' body (the phallus).

13) There is a substitution—Isis makes a substitute for the phallus.

14) There is a resurrection.

In the Masonic legend of Hiram Abiff, we find that:

1) There is the possession of something valuable—Hiram passed the Master's Word.

2) There is a conspiracy—fifteen Fellow Crafts conspire against Hiram.

3) There is a conflict—Hiram is attacked by Jubela, Jubelo and Jubelum at twelve noon.

4) There is a death—Hiram is killed by Jubelum.

5) Hiram's death was arranged by his brother.

6) The body is buried at the foot of a tamarind or arcacia tree.

7)   There is a first search—twelve Fellow
        Crafts search for the three murderers.

8)   They question everyone they meet.

9)   Their search is accidentally successful.

10)   There is a second search—three Fellow
        Crafts go in search of the body.

11)   There is a finding—the body is found in
        a grave dug due east and west.

12)   There is a loss—The Master's Word is
        lost.

13)   There is a substitution—"Mah-hah-bone"
        is the substitute.

14)   There is a resurrection—Hiram is raised
        from the grave.

**"The People of The Book know this
as they know their own sons, but
some of them conceal the Truth which
they themselves know." H.Q.**

Many of the Christian preachers and leaders have
been initiated into the so-called secrets of Freemasonry.
And they know that the story of Jesus Christ, as it is understood by the masses of the people, has its origin in mythology
and paganism; yet they will not educate their following
to this truth. The Hiramic legend is perhaps the most important story in the Masonic teachings. In order for a Mason
to be considered a Master, he must first be accepted and
initiated into the third degree wherein he is made to imitate
the legendary Hiram Abiff (who is also referred to as the
Widow's Son). Once the Mason reaches the 32nd degree,
he finds out, among other things, that the story of Hiram
Abiff actually refers and alludes to the story and life of
Jesus which is derived from the Osirian legend or myth,
as well as other ancient legends and pagan ideas.

According to the Masonic Ritual, the story of Hiram
Abiff is symbolic. In the 32nd degree (called the Sublime
Prince of the royal secret), it is said that <u>the symbolic mystery</u>

of the death of Hiram Abiff represents Jesus Christ. The three blows which were given to Hiram by Jubela, Jubelo and Jubelum at the three gates, acutally allude to the three points of condemnation against Jesus by the High Priest Caiphas, Herod and Pilate. "It was from the last that he was led to the most violent and excruciating death." They said three blows with the square, gauge and gavel, are symbols of the blow on the cheek, the flagellation and the crown of thorns. The brethren assembled around the tomb of Hiram is a representation of the disciples lamenting the death of Christ on the cross. The "Master's Word", which is said to be lost since the death of Hiram Abiff, is the same that Christ pronounced on the cross, and which the Jews did not comprehend: **"Eli, Eli, lama sabaethani?" ("My God, my God, why has thou forsaken me?"**); instead of which the words, **"Mah-hah-bone"(Welcome)"** were substituted. The false brethren represent Judas Iscariat, who sold Christ. The red collar worn by the Grand elect Perfect and Sublime Masons, calls to remembrance the blood of Christ. The sprig (of acacia) is the figure of the cross because from this wood was the cross made." (Richardson's Monitor of Freemasonry, p. 198). Hiram being buried on a hill refers to the supposed crucifixion of Jesus on the top of a hill. The resurrection of Hiram alludes to the resurrection and ascension of Jesus.

There is much more evidence which shows that the birth, death and resurrection of Jesus is connected to ancient mythology and paganism. Professor Hilton Hotema in his, Mystery Man of The Bible points out that the name Jesus Christ as well as his birth derived from the two sun gods called Hesus and Kristos. He writes,

"These gods were Hesus, worshipped to the west of Rome; and Kristos, worshipped to the east of Rome. Both had originated as symbols of the sun, but under the clever hand of the crafty priesthood had come to be considered as gods instead of symbols.... And why was the name Jesus linked with Kirstos from that time forward? To appease the worshippers of Hesus. This evidence shows that Jesus Christ of the New Testa-

-90-

ment is just a combination of the names of the
sun gods Hesus and Kristos."

Imam Warith Deen Muhammad, in speaking on the origin
of the Trinity, pointed out in a lecture entitled "Jain, Jacob
and Metaphysics" (1978), that the idea of God the father,
God the son and God the Holy Ghost, can be traced back
to Ancient Egypt. He said,

> "Horus, himself, is symbolic of God manifest
> in the world.... There is Horus the elder and
> Horus the young one. The elder is Osiris, the
> sun. Horus is the son of the sun. Now you have
> God the Father, you have Jesus the son of God,
> you have God in the Scripture depicted as a bright
> sun...and Jesus being the son of that sun. And
> Jesus said, 'I am the light of the world as long
> as I am in the world'... So you have this same
> kind of language—it is not a new language; it
> is a language from ancient Egypt."

Prophet Jesus was a righteous and faithful servant
of God. Muslims are obligated to accept Jesus Christ as
an Apostle of God. The Holy Qur'an says, "And in their
footsteps we sent Jesus the son of Mary, confirming the
Law that had come before him: We sent him the Gospel:
therein was guidance and light, and confirmation of the
Law that had come before him: A guidance and an admonition
to those who fear God" (5:49). Although Muslims believe
that Jesus was given divine revelation from God, the four
Gospels of the Bible are not generally accepted as that divine
revelation. The Bible contains much truth in it, but it is
hidden in symbolism and parables. In order to get some
light from the Bible, interpretation is required. Even though
the Bible was compiled by "the most trickiest men to ever
live," with the proper insight, much wisdom can be derived
from it; in its present state, however, it is as the Honorable
Elijah Muhammad said, "the graveyard of my people."

Jesus asked, "What man having a light would hide it
under a bushel basket?" He said, if you have a light, let
it shine. Now if it is true then that many Christian leaders

know the true history and meaning of the trinity, the imma-
culate conception, death and resurrection of Jesus, as well
as the other major Christian doctrines; if they know that
these concepts are derived from ancient mythology and
ancient pagan practices, but yet continue to preach and
teach the masses of people that Jesus is God, and God's
only begotten son, and that there is a trinity that forms
a Godhead, then they are hypocrites of the worst kind.
They are no less than dupes of the manipulators, conspirators
and devils.

What must we think of these Christian leaders who
come before the sincere and innocent Christian masses and
articulate this false propaganda after having, perhaps, been
initiated into the higher and secret wisdom of Christianity
(what the Rosicrucians call "Esoteric Christianity"); after
having received a deeper understanding of the Torah, the
Bible and certain aspects of the Holy Qur'an, and being initiated into the secrets of the Ancient Free and Accepted Scotch
or York Rite Order of Freemasonry, wherein they learn
that Christ is a state of consciousness that can be attained
by any human being, as well as other great moral truths
that would elevate and dignify humanity, they continue
to teach lies and fairy tales?

Considering the shameful, impoverished and ignorant
state of African-Americans and oppressed people everywhere,
it is a crime for anyone to bind himself to an oath that forbids
him from sharing knowledge with his people. Such individuals
are like unto the man who sold his soul for a bowl of parch;
he is a watchman for the slavemaster. Only a fool could
think that a people who denied you the opportunity to live
like a human being, enslaved your foreparents, oppressed,
mocked and scorned your people, would trust you with some
"grand secret"!

What does a Black man look like talking about he "got
some secret knowledge that he cannot share with his brethren
because he is not a Masonic brother who has 'crossed the
burning sands cable towed and blindfolded'"? History tells
us that African-Americans came to America with chains
around their necks and were made blind to the reality

of themselves as dignified human beings, and made to live under the heat of hatred and oppression. We have been in "distress" ever since we came here. If it were not for the mercy of God, perhaps we would have been completely destroyed. Now, if we can break the grip of white supremacy, ignorance and self-hatred, we would make imminent progress.

The preachers must stop preaching the fairy tale language of the Bible and start sharing the wisdom that is locked up in the Bible. If they do not know the hidden language of the Bible, then they should pick up the the Holy Qur'an, a pure and perfect book, and read it with a sincere heart so that they may receive guidance and learn wisdom.

Jesus said, "**Touch me not, I have not yet ascended.**" Jesus was a sign of the Word. The Bible says that he was "**The Word**" and he was crucified and buried. This tells us that <u>the truth or the message that Jesus brought was killed (corrupted) and buried under falsehood and materialism</u>. Therefore, if we want the pure message of Jesus, we have to wait until it ascends to the heavens—like the polluted water is raised to the heaven by the pull of the sun, made pure, and descends back down to the earth, fit to drink. "**Touch me not, I have not yet ascended.**" Prophet Muhammad ascended to the seventh heaven. The Holy Qur'an says the light came down with him. Prophet Muhammad never said, "Touch me not I have not yet ascended." He said that he "ascended", and in his vision he met several prophets (Jesus included) on various levels of the heaven. The Qur'an is not weighted with corruption, lies and supersititon. It is the "**clear evidence.**"

BIBLE LANGUAGE

Let us consider some of the language and terminology of the Bible and see if we can arrive at some knowledge and wisdom that could benefit our lives. If it holds true that the Bible, as most Christians believe, is a divinely revealed book, and according to Masonic language it is one of the "three great lights", then it should not be read with the same attitude of mind and spirit as other books are read. The Bible should be read with caution and strict examination. God speaks in a higher and more profound language than the human being. Therefore, in seeking the wisdom of God we should look deeper into the language of those scriptures (referring specifically to the Bible at this point), which we believe were revealed to man by God. In the Book of Matthew, it says, **"Whoso readeth, let him understand"** (24:15). This statement plainly tells us that it is not sufficient just to read and memorize the written word, it beckons us to search for higher understanding.

It is reported that King Solomon said, **"Wisdom is the principle thing; therefore get wisdom: And with all thy getting, get understanding."** In the word wisdom we see the words "wis" and "dom". The word dom has several references: (1) domain; (2) dominant; (3) dominion; (4) dome; (5) domestic, etc. Now if we rejoin the two words wiz and dom, and reflect on what Solomon said, we can see that he was saying "develop your mind; make enlightened your dome." Our head is the dome of our body or our dominion. A wise dome (mind) is essential for the protection and development of the human being.

"With all thy getting, get understanding." Let us look at the words, under and standing. Standing refers to that which is upright and obvious. Understanding, therefore, alludes to that which is beneath the obvious. It refers to the implicit or the hidden. It takes insight to see the implicit or hidden message. In Quranic language it is called **"taweel"**. If we look further at the word understanding and reverse

-94-

the prefix and the root, we get: standing under, which gives the same message or idea of "that which is under the surface or hidden."

Apparently Solomon understood the importance of education and insight. The Bible says that he did not pray for wealth or fame, but for wisdom and understanding. **"For wisdom is better than rubies; all the things that may be desired are not to be compared to it" (Proverbs 8:11). "Give therefore thy servant an understanding heart to judge thy people, that I may discern between good and bad; for who is able to judge this, thy so great a people"** (I Kings 3:9).

In searching for insight and an intelligent understanding of the Bible, the Christian theologians have established two very important principles or methods of interpreting the Bible. The first one is called **"Hermeneutics,"** and it refers to "the methodological principles of interpreting the Bible". The other principle is called **"Exegesis"**, and it refers to the actual explanation or critical interpretation of the Bible. It should be noted that many of the Christian leaders do not accept the literal translation of the Bible.

THE CALL TO EDUCATION AND ENLIGHTENMENT

The Bible gives us two pictures of the beginning. In Genesis it says, **"In the beginning God created the heavens and the earth, and the earth was without form and void, and darkness was upon the face of the deep. And the Spirit of God moved upon the face of the waters. And God said, 'let there be light', and there was light"** (1:1-4). In the Gospel according to John, it reads, **"In the beginning was the word, and the word was with God, and the word was God... In Him was life; and the life was the light of men. And the light shineth in darkness; and the darkness comprehended it not"** (1:1, 3-5).

In both these verses we are encouraged to develop our minds and to seek enlightenment. As human beings we come into this world ignorant to the environment. After being in the darkness of our mother's womb for approximately nine months, we come into another world of darkness. Although the physical environment may be lit with the light of knowledge, as well as the sunlight and man-made fluorescent light, the darkness of experience still dominates the mind of that new born baby. As the human being begins to grow, his mind feeds from the signs or words of the environment and pretty soon he comes into the knowledge (light) of his environment. **"In the beginning was the word."** When we come into this world, the signs or words of creation are already here. The Bible tells us that God created the physical environment before he created the human being. The Bible says he placed Adam in the Garden. The Garden was already there. A garden is a place for growth.

Light enables us to see and move around in the world with a sense of security. Likewise for knowledge. It enables us to see the traps and pitfalls of society as well as the positive things that exist in society and in ourselves. Knowledge enables us to see and appreciate the mercy and compassion of God. It enables us to see the great gifts and signs of His precious creation. According to Genesis, God told Adam that he could eat from every society (tree) except the one that bore the fruit of the <u>knowledge of good and evil.</u> If the tree in the midst of the garden bore the knowledge of good and evil, then what kind of knowledge did the other tree bare? It is apparent that the other trees (societies) either bore the fruit of the knowledge of all good or all bad, but not both. The All Wise and Perfect Creator would not tell his human being to eat from a tree (society) that bore the fruit of corrupt knowledge; therefore, when He said, **"eat from every tree"** He was instructing us to feed and develop our minds with truth and pure knowledge. In explaining the tree as a symbol of society, Imam Warith Deen Muhammad pointed out,

> "The tree as a symbol of society speaks to the development of society. Society feeds from the earth for its material development like a tree gets water out of the earth to feed its body.

A tree that gets no water soon withers, its limbs weaken and droop, and it is soon dead. The roots of the tree go down deep in the earth searching for water, so that the tree can live even if the rain does not come. Society is also like this. When man forms society, he does not like to wait until some natural happening brings food into his environment. Man will go dig up the earth and till the ground so that he will have food even if the heavens do not 'bless' him. The society of man, like the tree, sows its roots deep in the earth.

"The body of the tree has the strength of the tree because the trunk holds up the high branches that stretch out with great weight. Water goes through the body and feeds the leaves. In the very top of the tree there is also a kind of feeding taking place. The tree feeds from beneath and it feeds from above. The leaves, which feed on sunlight and carbon dioxide, produce oxygen like human beings feed on oxygen and produce carbon dioxide. The leaves of the tree feed from above, and the roots of the tree feed from below. Because the tree is a life that feeds from the material body and also from the heavenly body, the ancients saw it as a very good picture of the human society. There are some people who feed first from the ground, and there are other people who feed from things that are above the ground, from higher moral values, from the light of God, and from righteousness." (Lectures of Imam Muhammad, p. 45, 47).

So the human being was permitted to eat or learn from every society except the one in the midst of the garden that produced a deceptive fruit or deceptive knowledge. Any society that produces a fruit of the knowledge of good and evil is a corrupt and deceitful society. It is like a wolf in sheep's clothing. This kind of tree (society) gives us a fruit (body of knowledge) that looks good and attractive on the outside, but underneath the surface is poison, lies, corrupt knowledge and death. God said, "Oh man don't eat from that tree (society) because it is unfit for consumption." But He also inspired Prophet Muhammad (PBUH) to say, "seek wisdom from the cradle to the grave" and, "Go in quest of knowledge even unto China, even unto the edge of the earth." (Thus Spoke Prophet Muhammad). Allah says in the Holy Qur'an that there are signs in the creation for those who have understanding.

So we see that the Scripture is calling us to knowledge. The Scripture is telling the human being to grow in knowledge and wisdom. The Bible says, **"In the beginning was the word."** This statement is not necessarily referring to the spoken word as much as it is referring to the words or signs in creation. When we observe creation, we see signs that speak to our minds like words. Before man developed the written language, he used signs and symbols as a means of expression and communication. A word is anything that brings a message to the mind. Historians and Egyptologists have discovered and interpreted much of the sign language that was used by the Ancient Egyptians and others. This sign language was called, hieroglyphics. When the Book says, **"The Word was with God and it is God"**, it is reminding us that when we look at the universe, we see one word. Although these are narrow parts in the creation, they all work together as one unit. Thus we have the word, universe (which means one sign). Again, we have two eyes but one vision or focus; two ears, but we hear one sound; two nostrils, but one smell. God tells us in the Holy Qur'an that the creation is bigger than man. It also tells us that **"His grasp is over all things"**. In other words, we cannot see outside of this physical creation. The signs or words of Allah (God) are all around us and they speak to our inner being by way of our senses. **"And the Word was with God."** This tells us that, although we cannot see the Creator in His totality, when we look at the physical creation, we see His workings which are an expression or manifestation of His will. Therefore, in the magnificent and marvelous creation, we can see signs of the compassion and the excellence of the Creator.

"And the word was made flesh" (John 1:14). As the human mind grows and begins to analyze what it sees, it deciphers and categorizes the signs, symbols, colors, etc. that are being observed. It begins to <u>reason</u> and learn that "All that glitters is not gold" or the only thing green is not grass. According to Dr. Na'im Akbar, "Reason brings order and organization to the information brought in by the senses. With reason we know that everything that is green is not grass. With reason we know that our senses give us incomplete information about the world. With reason we also use time to help us make effective judgements. We are able to distinguish between yesterday's experience and today's reality. We are equipped with reason to classify experiences in terms of time, space,, quality, and other dimensions. Reason gives meaning or interpretation to experience." <u>(Community of Self,</u> p. 8).

The mind "eats" the words or signs of the environment. "You are what you eat." Our minds feed on the environment and internalizes the messages that are given, which mold and shape our mind, behavior and personality. Sociologists agree that we are a product of our environment. It is reported that Jesus said, **"Man cannot live by bread alone, but by every word that proceedth out of the mouth of the Lord."** These words become a part of the human being. According to the Hermetic Philosophy, there is a consistent correspondence between the physical creation and the mind of man. This is called "The Principle of Correspondence" and it alludes to the axiom, "as above, so below; as below, so above." (The Kybalion, p. 28). The Holy Qur'an says, **"Allah it is Who hath created seven heavens, and of the earth the like thereof."** (85:12). It is also important to understand that the ancient Masters taught that the outer world is an expression of the inner world of man and visa versa. The mass of physical creation is called the macrocosm, and the human being is called the microcosm. They taught, "that which is on the outside is also in the inside." In other words, the words or signs in the physical creation become flesh in man, they are consumed by man, who is both flesh and spirit.

-99-

"**The word became flesh**" is telling us that once the human being reads the signs in creation and interprets those signs, digests them, and uses them to elevate himself, the words become flesh. Also, when we read the scripture, we are actually eating the words of God. What we eat becomes a part of us. In the Book of Jeremiah we read where the Prophet says, he ate the words of God. "**Thy words were found, and I did eat them.**" (15:16). This is referring to the same idea that is expressed in the statement, "**The word was made flesh.**" God has commanded us to get knowledge that we may grow, mentally, morally and spiritually.

The Bible, Genesis says, "**In the beginning was darkness.**" What does that mean? It means that the human being was/is first a creation of faith. When we came into the world as babies, without knowledge of the environment, our faith and trust is in our parents, for food, love, affection. In early states we do not move by the light of knowledge; but by faith. Faith leads us to knowledge. Darkness tests our faith. For example, if you were put into a strange and new environment, your sense of security would be threatened and you would have to depend on the truthfulness of those in that environment. It is like asking someone for direction to a certain place or street. Likewise, the young mind feels its way around in darkness, dependent on its parents to feed and protect it. Imam Warith Deen Muhammad says, "Darkness makes us come together. As long as we have some light we may remain selfishly independent. We might try to use our little light to gain an advantage over others. But if the light goes out and total darkness prevails, people start to fear being alone, and they begin to sense the need for trust among themselves." (Prayer and Al-Islam, p. 65). Faith is essential in human development and religion. So although darkness usually refers to ignorance and corruption, it also refers to the need for faith.

In referring to the early stages of human societal development in darkness (ignorance), the Bible says that Adam (a society of people), was naked (Genesis 5:1-2). But he did not become aware and ashamed of his nakedness until he received knowledge. Naked means uncultured, unrefined and primitive. Again, it refers to the early stage of human development. The baby comes here without knowledge and mental refinement. Society starts out uncultured, unrefined and primitive (superstitious). Allah (God) says in the Holy Qur'an that only after He has duly proportioned his man, would the angels be obligated to bow down to him. In the early history of man, we find that he bowed and worshipped the angels (forces in creation) because he was ignorant and superstitious. Once the human being grew in knowledge, wisdom and understanding and love for the true Creator, he was then able to master and control some of the angels (forces in creation). As long as man was naked, he feared the angels (forces in nature, i.e. thunder, lightening, rain, snow, etc.). In fact, history tells us that primitive man worshipped many of these forces as God. The Bible says when the early man (mind) heard the thunder he became afraid and hid himself. It reads, **"And he (Adam) said, I heard thy voice in the garden, and I was afraid, because I was naked; and I hid myself."** (Genesis 3:10). The Bible also says that He made his man a little below the angels. **"But we see Jesus, who was made a little lower than the angels"** (Hebrew 2:9). In Christianity, Jesus is called the second Adam, which only means that he is an expression of the first Adam.

Nakedness represents crewdness. It alludes to the first stage of human and societal development. The same message is also given in the Biblical story of Noah. It says, **"And he drank of the wine and was drunken; and he was uncovered within his tent."** (Genesis 9:21). Noah also represents the beginning of a world. The Bible says, the old world was destroyed by water and God started a new world with Noah and his family. Noah was not drunk from wine, but he was overtaken by the spirit of God just like Adam. Adam went into a deep sleep, so did Noah. Adam did not know he was naked until he became conscious, likewise with Noah, he did not know that he was naked until he gained consciousness. Noah was naked, only means that he did not have culture, because he and his family was in a new environment, that society was in its primitive stages. Noah had no knowledge of the physical environment because he had just travelled from the old world to the new world, like the new-born baby comes from the world of its mother's anatomy to the outer world of man. The Qur'an says, **"Verily in this is a sign: but most of them do not believe."** (23:30). Noah had not yet eaten (learned) the words (knowledge) of the new environment. So, dear brothers and sisters, let us seek diligently knowledge and understanding.

The Holy Prophet Muhammad (PBUH) said, "He who leaveth home in search of knowledge, walketh in the path of God." He also said, "Whoever seeketh knowledge and findeth it, will get two rewards; one of them the reward for desiring it, and the other for attaining it; therefore, even if he does not attain it, for him is one reward." (Thus Spoke Prophet Muhammad, p.46,47). Once we are soundly rooted in knowledge, we will be able to compete intelligently and not emotionally with the other races in the world. We are a people who were made naked and deprived of the light of culture and human intelligence. The deceivers and oppressors gave us a false idea of God and ourselves. The Bible says, **"Adam and his wife (society) covered themselves with the leaves to hide their shame."** Leaves are symbolic of "leaves of a book," which are the pages of the book. This refers to the ideology and philosophy that dominates society. For example, in America, the dominating idea is capitalism and democracy. The constitution is the document by which this country is governed. We were given a page from the book of white supremacy in the form of corrupt Christianity and fairy tale language, to cover our nakedness. Allah tells us in the Holy Qur'an that he gave Adam the garments of righteousness to cover his shame. The Masons claim that the leaves that Adam covered himself with refers to the Masonic Apron that is worn by its members. "It is an emblem of innocence and a badge of of a Mason."

Concerning the Word, the Masons and Shriners claim that it was lost at the building of Solomon's Temple. They are looking for the Logos or the "Lost Word." They are "traveling and searching for the light and that which was lost." They understand the "light" to mean knowledge and Divine Truth. But they are also looking for a Word, that was lost. It is called the Sacred Word or the Secret Word.

Bibliography

1. Huber L. Drumright, Ph.D., Introducing The Bible, King James Version, p. 8.

2. Muhammad Ata Ur-Rahim, Jesus, A Prophet of Islam, MWH, London Publishers, London 1977, p. 39.

3. The Gospel of Barnabas, edited and translated by Lansdale and Laura Ragg, p. 59-59.

4. Huber L. Drumuright, opt.cit., p. 6.

5. Ulfat Us-Samad, A Comparative Study of Christianity and Islam, S.H. Muhammad Ashraf, Lahore Pakistan, 1974, p. 15.

6. Maurice Bucaille, The Bible The Quran and Science, Sighers Publishers, Paris France, 1982, p. 133-4.

7. Muhammad Ata Ur-Rahim, opt. cit., p. 12.

8. Ibid., p. 80.

9. Rev. Robert Taylor A.D. and M.R.C.S., The Diegisis, p. 351.

10. Imam Alauddin Shabazz, The Plain Truth About the Birth of Jesus According to the Holy Bible, New Mind Productions, Jersey City, NJ, 1981, p. 16-17.

FREEMASONRY

The Great Seal of the United States

FREEMASONRY

Before proceeding with our last section, it is important that we mention that one of the reasons we felt it was necessary to write about Freemasonry in connection with Al-Islam and Christianity is primarily due to the fact that Freemasonry, as a system, incorporates many of the ideas and practices of both religions. In addition, although Freemasonry claims it promotes religious tolerance, much evidence has been presented by worthy authors to show that it underminds the basic beliefs of both religions. Muhammad Safwat Al-Saqqa Amini and Sa'di Abu Habib in their book, Freemasonry, writes, "In the dialogue of the thirtieth degree it is noted that, 'Muhammad (God bless him and grant him salvation) is an alleged prophet, who, with Christ, is the archenemy of mankind's faith; and that the glorious Qur'an is a branch of the Torah.'"

Rev. Martin L. Wagner points out that, "The most dangerous antagonists of Christianity in its earliest days were the worship of Isis, under various modifications as Demeter, Cybele Diana, or as the power of fertility; and Mithraism, the worship of the generative power under the aspect of light. The enemies of Christianity clothed these ideas in the language of the New Testament and the Church.... By skillfully veiling pagan ideas under the terminology of Christian doctrine, many who thought themselves serving the Lord Jesus Christ were led unconsciously into the pagan cults. And this is the method of Freemasonry." (Freemasonry an Interpretation, p. 19-20). **Furthermore, it is our caution to the striving poor whether Muslim or Christian, that they be aware of certain hidden forces that are present and have their influences in our lives. It is particularly important to those of us who are seeking to advance ourselves and our people politically, economically and morally.** This is not to say, however, that Freemasonry alone is the arch-enemy of religion and mankind, but it has been used as a tool by evil-minded individuals to gain world dominance. According to the Scottish Rite Ritual, "Masonry will eventually rule the world."

History tells us of one Adam Weishaupt who on May 1, 1776 founded the "Illuminati" system, after which he and his followers infiltrated the Masonic system. Webster writes, "From the moment of Weishaupt's admission into Freemasonry, his whole conduct was a violation of the Masonic code. Instead of proceeding after the recognized manner by successive stages of initiation, he set himself to find out further secrets by underhanded methods and then to turn to the advantage of his own system." She further points out that, "Weishaupt's followers were enlisted by the most subtle methods of deception..." (Secret Societies and Subversive Movements, p. 198,209).

We read in The Protocols of the Learned Elders of Zion of a plan to use the Masonic lodges for subversive aims: "Meantime, however, until we come into our kindgom, we shall act in the contrary way: we shall create and multiply free masonic lodges in all the countries of the world, absorb into them all who may become or who are prominent in public activity, for those lodges we shall find our principle intelligence office and means of influence...In these lodges we shall tie together the knot which binds together all revolutionary and liberal elements. Their composition will be made up of all strata of society. The most secret political plots will be known to us and fall under our guiding hands on the very day of their conception." (p.53). Buck writes, "The most profound secrets of Masonry are not revealed in the Lodge at all. They belong only to the few." (Mystic Masonry XXVI).

There are many reasons why Freemasonry and secret societies should be shunned by God-conscious people and civilized society; but the main reason why they should be rejected and condemned by Muslims is best stated in the Holy Qur'an: "In most of their secret talks there is no good." (4:114) Allah also says, "**They may hide (their crimes) from men, but they cannot hide (them) from Allah, seeing that He is in their midst when they plot by night, in words that He cannot approve: and Allah doth compass round all that they do.**" (4:108).

From my research, I have come to see that Masonry uses (in addition to its symbolism) very beautiful and charming language. At first glance it appears as if it is a "a lamb with neither spot nor blemish." Claiming as its goal the advancement and enlightenment of all humanity, Freemasonry seeks to appeal to the "truth seekers" on the one hand, by dangling in front of them the words of the Scripture; while on the other hand it appeals to the materialists and power seekers through its great intrigue of secrecy. To say, however, that deep in the dark chambers of Masonry there lies no truth and principles of goodness, would be totally false and unfair. To say that the system is "one giant evil" would be perhaps naive. On the contrary, to say as Harold W. Percival writes, "There are no better and no more advanced teachings available to human beings than those of Masonry," is ludicrous.

DEFINITION AND PURPOSE OF FREEMASONRY

Masonic scholars and writers differ on the exact meaning of term Freemasonry. Some argue that Freemasonry is a system of morality and spiritual advancement. Mackey defines it as a "science which is engaged in divine truth, and which employs symbolism as its method of instruction. Freemasonry, says Buck, "is a summary of human wisdom, clear, concise and simple, such as nowhere exists in the world." Hemming writes, "According to the general acceptation of the term, is an art founded on the principles of geometry and directed to the service and convenience of mankind." Buck also argues that Freemasonry is "the 'universal religion' only because, and only so long as it embraces all religions." He further explains "Masonry is not only a universal science, but a world-wide religion, and owes allegiance to no one creed, and can adopt no sectarian dogma as such without ceasing thereby to be Masonic." Still another writer defines Freemasonry as, "friendship, love and integrity."

Perhaps the most widely accepted definition of Freemasonry is that of Albert Pike. He writes, "Freemasonry is the subjugation of the human that is in man by the divine; the conquest of the appetites and passions by the moral sense and the reason; a continual effort, struggle, and warfare of the spiritual against the material and sensual." (Morals and Dogma, p. 854).

A definition can also be derived from the very word Freemasonry itself. The word **"free"** means **"without hinderance or restriction"**. The word **"mason"** refers to **"one who builds, a brick layer"**. Masonry is that system or art of building or brick laying (stonework or brickwork). It should be noted that there are **two kinds of Masonry**. First there is **"operative masonry"** which concerns itself with the physical act of building or construction. The second type of masonry is called **"specultative masonry"** which refers to the process or act of building a spiritual or mental edifice within the human being. It alludes to the art of building character, erecting the human intellect in an upright posture. In addition, it refers to the science of erecting the human society based on the principles of truth, justice and morality. Therefore it can be concluded that the term Freemason(ry) means **"one who is free to build a physical or mental and spiritual edifice"**. In fact, according to the Masonic Ritual, before a person can become a Freemason, he must first be a "free man". "A slave cannot be a Mason." Percival writes, "In a wider sense, he must not be a slave to lust and avarice" (Masonry and its Symbols, p. 7).

The purpose of Freemasonry, writes one author, is to train a human being so that he will reconstruct, through the body of change and death which he now has, a perfect physical body which shall not be subject to death. The plan is to build this deathless body, called by modern Masons, King Solomon's Temple, out of material in the physical body, which is called the ruins of Solomon's Temple. The plan is to build a temple not made with hands, eternal in the heavens, which is the cryptic name for the deathless physical vesture.

It is further claimed that the purpose of Freemasonry is to lead mankind to freedom and enlightenment. Pike states that, "it is also the duty of Masonry to assist in elevatinj the moral and intellectual level of society, in gaining knowledge, bringing ideas into circulation, and causing the mind of youth to grow; and in putting gradually, by the teachings of axioms and the promulgation of positive laws, the human race in harmony with its destinies." He further argues that the aim of Masonry, "which is ordained by God," is "to bestow on its adherents manhood, science and philosophy". Pike also claims that, "it is the province of Masonry to teach all truth--not moral truth alone, but political and philosophical, and even religious truth, so far as concerns the great and essential principles of each." Timothy Tindal Robertson, in his book, Freemasonry and the Vatican, quotes certain masonic authorities as stating, "Freemasonry claims to have an aim which is progressive, philanthropic and humanitarian. It seeks to guide the moral and spiritual development of humanity outside and above any differences of class, nationality or creed... Its aims are the search for truth, the study of morality and the practice of solidarity. It works for human betterment both materially and morally, and for the social and intellectual perfecting of man." On page 153 of the book, Morals and Dogma, it reads, "It is not the mission of Masonry to engage in plots and conspiracies against the civil government. It is not the fanatical propagandist of any creed or theory; nor does it proclaim itself the enemy of kings. It is the apostle of liberty, equality, and fraternity."

Why, then, the strict secrecy? Why the rigorous initiations? Robertson says, "there must then be something else. In fact, these attractive sounding principles have been very cleverly drawn up in order to conceal profoundly subversive activities under a cover of pleasing vagueness." One of the major objectives of Freemasonry is to bring man from darkness to light and to raise the human's mind from a "dead level to a living perpendicular." Newton in his book, The Builders, explains Freemasonry as, "gentle, gracious and wise." "Its mission," he says, "is to form mankind into a great redemptive brotherhood, a league of noble and free men enlisted in the radiant enterprise of working out, in time, the love and will of God." He continues "Earnestly it (Freemasonry) endeavors to bring men—first the individual man, and then, so far as possible, those who are united with him—to love one another while holding aloft, in picture and dream, that temple of character which is the noblest labor of life to build in the midst of years, and which will outlast time and death. Thus it seeks to reach the lonely inner life of man where the real battles are fought, and where the issues of destiny are decided, now with shouts of victory, now with sobs of defeat...Here lies the great secret of Masonry—that it makes a man aware of that divinity within him, wherefrom his whole life takes its beauty and meaning and inspires him to follow and obey it: making his existence a process of self-discovery, self-mastry, and self-spending."

We should ask ourselves, if the aim of Freemasonry is (according to Masonic authority) to advance, unify and enlighten humanity, why the secrecy? If its goal is to help the human family, why not let us know publicly how it intends to help us. Does not it seem rather suspicious that on the one hand Freemasonry claims to promote human enlightenment, but its members are restricted to the most rigorous secrecy, under the most brutal death oaths. From the first degree to the last, the Mason is reminded of his sworn oath of secrecy. For example, in the first degree (called Entered Apprentice) the following oath is taken upon the Bible Square and Compass:

Oath:

I_____, of my own free will and accord, in the presence of Almighty God and this Worshipful Lodge, erected to Him and dedicated to the Saints John, do hereby and hereon most solemnly and sincerely promise and swear, that I will always hail, <u>ever conceal, and never reveal</u> any of the secret arts, parts or points of the hidden mysteries of ancient Freemasonry, which have been heretofore, may at this time, or shall at any future period, be communicated to me as such, to any person or persons whomsoever, except it be to a true and lawful brother of this degree... I furthermore promise and swear that I will not write, paint, stamp, stain, cut, carve, mark, nor engrave them, nor cause the same to be done upon anything movable or immovable, capable of receiving the least impression of a word, syllable, letter or character, whereby the same may become legible or intelligible to any person under the canopy of heaven.

"All of this I most solemnly and sincerely promise and swear, with a firm and steadfast resolution, to keep and perform the same without any equivocation, mental reservation or secret evasion of mind whatever, <u>binding myself under a no less penalty than that of having my throat cut across, my tongue, torn out by its roots and buried in the rough sands of the sea at low water mark,</u>

<u>where the tide ebbs and flows, twice in twenty-four</u>
<u>hours, should I, in the least knowledge or wittingly</u>
<u>violate or transgress, this my solemn obligation</u>
<u>of an Entered Apprentice Mason. So help me</u>
<u>God, and keep me steadfast."</u>

In the second degree, he swears that he will not reveal anything he has learned under "no less a penalty than that of having my left breast torn open, my heart plucked out and given as a prey to the beast of the field and the fowls of the air." In the third degree, he binds himself under no less penalty than that of having "my body cut in two, my bowels taken from thence and burned to ashes, and the ashes scattered to the four winds of heaven, that no trace or rememberance may be had of so vile and perjured a wretch as I."

In the thirteenth degree, the Mason agrees among other things, **"to keep exactly in my heart all the secrets that shall be revealed to me. And in failure of this my oath, I consent to have my body opened perpendicularly, and to be exposed for eight hours in the open air that the venomous flies may eat of my intestines, my head to be cut off and put on the highest pinnacle of the world, and I will always be ready to inflict the same punishment on those who shall disclose this degree and break this oath. So may God help and maintain me. Amen."**

In the twenty-eighth degree, he says **"May my brethren seize me and thrust my tongue through with red hot iron, to pluck out my eyes and deprive me of smelling and seeing, to cut off my hands and expose me in that condition in the field to be devoured by the voracious animals, and if none can be found, may the lightening of heaven execute on me the same vengence. So may God maintain me in rightousness and equity. Amen."**

Many may argue that these penalties are merely symbolic. That may be true. However, it still serves as a deterrent to free expression by masons concerning those things that they are taught in the lodge. It is a known fact that secrecy is considered essential for the preservation of Masonry. Mackey points out that secrecy is one of the most important landmarks of Masonry. In Robertson's book we read the following quotes, **"Masonry should be felt everywhere, but nowhere should it be unveiled."** (Convent of the Grand Orient, 1922, p.362.) "The whole strength of Masonry lies in its discretion. Our enemies fear us all the more because we never reveal our methods of action."

Returning our attention again to the aims and purpose of Freemasonry, we find that it presents for itself a noble purpose. On the surface it is quite enticing. And it is this very enticement, as well as its air of mystery, that attracts so many people to its door. The Bible tells us of a tree that bore the fruit of the knowledge of good and evil. On the surface, the fruit was appealing to the eye, it looked so sweet and appetizing, until Adam and Eve disobeyed the command of God just to taste that knowledge, only to find out that under the surface was corruption, falsehood and ignorance. Deception is the way of Satan. The Holy Qur'an says, "But Satan promises them nothing but deceit." (17:64).

We are of the opinion that Freemasonry along with many other secret societies is designed to hold the precious knowledge of scripture and human nature from the masses, for the purpose of ruling the masses. Based on the teachings of Jesus as presented in the Bible, Freemasonry is unChristian, and based on the profound words of Allah (God) as it is revealed in the Holy Qur'an, Freemasonry and its secrecy is unIslamic. Allah commanded us through the Prophet Muhammad (PBUH) to teach the truth openly and plainly.

ORIGIN OF FREEMASONRY

It has often been said that history is most qualified to reward all researchers. Bearing this in mind, we will now turn our attention to the history of Freemasonry, in hopes that we will be rewarded with the fruits of knowledge, for our labor. Concerning the History of Freemasonry, we find that its origin is shrouded in obscurity. This is primarily due to the fact that it (freemasonry) as we know it today has its roots planted in both authentic facts and unauthentic traditions or legends. In referring to its philosophy, its symbols and emblem, most Masonic authorities claim that freemasonry goes back to the ages of "remote antiquity." One Masonic author writes "The Order existed under one or another as a compact, well organized body long before the building of the oldest pyramid." He asserts that it is older than any religion known today. Freemasonry, he writes, and the system of its teaching "with the tools, landmarks, emblems and symbols, have always been substantially the same. It goes back to the age when bodies became male and female." (Masonry and its Symbols, p. 1-2). Alluding to the same assertion, Albert Pike, (one of Masonry's most prominent scholars) points out that the traditions, philosophy and symbols go to the creation of the first man, and even farther. He writes, "With her traditions reaching back to the earliest times, and her symbols dating farther back than even the monumental history of Egypt extends...it is still that which it was in the cradle of the human race, when no human foot had trodden to soil of Assyria and Egypt, and no colonies had crossed the Himalayas into Southern India, Media or Etrusia." These claims of antiquity are easily and readily made by Masons simply because of the double nature of that institution. Oftentimes the spiritual or philosophical history of Freemasonry is confused with the actual origin of its institution. It is easy , for example, for Pike or Percival to state that Freemasonry goes back to the most ancient times, simply because Freemasonry as a philosphy and an organization had adopted and intertwined the wisdom, practices and customs of various philosophies and religions into its own doctrine and claimed it as its own.

Therefore, if you find any truth in the Bible, the Mason says "that's Masonry." If a Muslim expounds upon the science of Al-Islam that science is called "Masonry". Some Masonic writers have went as far as to say Adam was a mason because the Bible says he covered his private area with leaves which represent the "Masonic apron". Such claims are made by those who want to make the uninitiated think that the "wisdom of the ages" can only be found in Masonry. One discredited Masonic historian argues that the lodge began with creation itself and that Adam was not only the first man but the first Masonic Grand Master. (Christianity and American Freemasonry, p. 13). Who made him "Grand Master"? Who taught Adam? Was it the chief officer of the Lodge seated in the East or was it God the Creator of All things, the All Wise One? According to the Holy Qur'an, Allah (God) taught Adam and blessed him with guidance (2:31). and the Bible says God said, **"Let there be light."** And God made the man "crown of creation." Whalen tells us that "Modern Masonry has borrowed from many diverse traditions such as those of the supressed Knights Templar, the Roman Collegia of Artifices, the Jewish Kabbalists, the mystery cults, the Rosicrucians and the operative Masons of the Middle Ages."

Several noted and respected Masonic historians have given a more candid and fair assessment of the origin of Masonic philosophy. Durrah explains: "Masons have believed the things concerning the origin of the institution that they wanted to believe, and have gone forth and told them as facts. when links were missing, they have been supplied by drawing upon fertile imaginations." He continues, "If there is in Freemasonry any similarity between its customs and those of the practices of several thousand years ago, it does not mean that Freemasonry has any connection whatsoever with those rites, but that they were woven into the fraternity in modern times with a view to enhancing the ritual and investing the fraternity with an atmosphere of antiquity (History and Evolution of Freemasonry, p. 25, 35).

Johnston informs us that "Modern Freemasonry, the creation of deists and Jews with a measure of Huguenot assistance, built on a foundation provided by the old confraternities of stonemasons, which in a degenerate form had survived the Reformation." (Freemasonry, a Short Historical Sketch, p. 3). Pike and Knight agree that Freemasonry is a concoction of various ideologies and has not its origins rooted in the remotest of antiquity. They confess that, "many of the doctrines or tenants inculcated in Freemasonry belong to the vast traditions of humanity of all ages and all parts of the world. Nevertheless, not only has no convincing evidence yet been brought forward to prove the lineal descent from any ancient organization...From what we know of the craft in the few centuries prior to the formation of the first Grand Lodge in 1717, it is excessively unlikely that there was any such parentage." (The Pocket History of Freemasonry, p. 9).

Perhaps the reader has thought that Freemasonry originated from ancient times and that it is an ancient organization. I am sure this is partly due to the fact that the largest and most powerful Masonic organization, Scottish Rite, bears the name "Ancient" and Accepted Scottish Rite or Ancient Free and Accepted Masons. The only thing that is ancient about Freemasonry is the fact that it uses the signs, symbols, emblems, customs, etc. of ancient times. Freemasonry, as it is known today in terms of its institutions, is not ancient, and Most Masonic Scholars agree on that point. In fact, Dr. Albert G. Mackey, a Masonic author and Historian, who was not only a thirty-third degree Mason, but as a contributor to the literature and science of Freemasonry, is recognized as having done more extensive work on the subject of Masonry than any other in America or Europe. Dr. Mackey explains in the Encyclopedia of Freemasonry that he once held the opinion that Modern Masonry was ancient, but through further investigation he learned quite the contrary.

He states, "Years ago in writing an article on this subject under the impressions made upon me by the fascinating theories of Dr. Oliver, though I never completely accepted his views, I was led to place the organization of Freemasonry, as it now exists, at the building of Solomon's Temple. Many years of subsequent research have led me greatly to modify the views I had previously held...I confess that I cannot find any incontrovertible evidence that would trace Freemasonry, as now organized, beyond the building corporations of the Middle Ages.

"The theory, then, that I advance on the subject of the antiquity of Freemasonry is this: I maintain that, in its present peculiar organization, it is the successor, with certainty, of the building corporations of the Middle Ages, and through them, with less certainty but with great probability, of the Roman colleges of artifices. Its connection with the Temple of Solomon as its birthplace may have been accidental--a mere arbitrary selection by its inventors--and bears, therefore, only an allegorical meaning; or it may be historical, and can be explained by the frequent communications that at one time took place between the Jews and the Greeks and the Romans... The historical materials upon which to base an opinion are as yet too scanty. But I am inclined, I confess, to view the Temple of Jerusalem and the Masonic tradiitons connected with it as a part of the great allegory of Freemasonry." He continues, "But as a secret association, containing within itself the symbolic expression of a religious idea, it connects itself with all the ancient mysteries, which, with similar secrecy, gave the same symbolic expression to the same religious idea. These mysteries were not the cradles of Freemasonry: they were only its analogies." In his conclusion, he adds, "And so, when I speak of the antiquity of Freemasonry, I must say, if I would respect the axioms of historical science, that its body came out of the Middle Ages, and that its spirit is to be traced to a far remote period." (p. 77-88).

It should be clear to us now that according to Masonic writers and historians, that the Masonic institution is modern but its mysteries, emblems, symbolism, etc. are adopted from the ancient mysteries and customs of various nations. It could be reasoned that the Masonic system is designed to teach its initiates the ancient mysteries and to inspire them to seek the wisdom and meaning of the ancient symbols, as well as the precious jewels of knowledge that exists in the various ideological philosophies and religions throughout the world. According to Masonic teachings each member is considered a "traveler" who is seeking light (knowledge). The ritual says, the Mason travels from west to east in search of "light" or the "lost word". Can it be true that perhaps the lodges were originally established in the West, Europe and America, to house the wisdom of the prophets from the East?

According to most Masonic writers and historians the first Grand Lodge was established in England in the year 1717. Masons, who are also symbolically called "sons of light", consider the East as the source of knowledge and wisdom. According to the Shriners' wisdom, the understanding, insight and the keys to the symbols of ancient Egypt, are in Makkah. On page 9 of the Ancient Arabic Order of the Nobles of the Mystic Shrine: Its History and Pleasures, it reads, "In imitation of the humility of the wisest of mankind, we look to the East for light, and find placed there the beautiful emblem of newborn light, the crescent." The Shriners' ritual states that certain individuals from the west went to Makkah and received "the secret work" and brought it back to America and established Shriners' Temples throughout the Western Hemisphere (The Secret Ritual of the Ancient Arabic Order of Nobles of the Masonic Shrine, p. 5-7).

On page 16 of the History and Pleasures, we read, "We thus commemorate the inspired prophecy announced at Makkah centuries ago, with the transformation of 'The Adoration' or The Keys of Secret Knowledge, 'The Inevitable', 'The Rending Asunder', of Al-Koran, and the final individualization of the soul and the recognition of Allah the Most High." The Shriners' pass word is "Makkah." It is no doubt that the ignorant and evil-minded Mason and Shriner use the Shriners' organization to mock the religion of Al-Islam, but there are those who also see the greatness of this universal religion, learn its wisdom, respect its principles and honor the Prophet. Nevertheless, it still stands, according to their writings, that the land where the Prophets traveled and lived is where the knowledge of the great secrets existed. Imam W. Deen Muhammad, in his book Imam W. Deen Muhammad Speaks From Harlem, New York, explains: "So actually, all of this science we are talking about, it goes back to the oldest house, Al-Baitul Aqib, the Kaabah and the people who lived in that vicinity. The Shriners know this, the higher ups in the Christian sciences, they know this. They know that their sciences did not come from Egypt. They are highly excited by all the mythology in Egypt. And instead of accepting the human disciplines that are contained in the science of the oldest science in Makkah, they got some insight from the Makkan occult sciences, and they went to Egypt to decipher that symbolism with the tools of Makkah. They went to Egypt to decipher the symbolism." (p. 124-25).

Nesta H. Webster writes, "The East is the cradle of secret societies. For whatever end they may have been employed, the inspiration and methods of those mysterious associations which have played so important a part behind the scene of the world's history will be founded to have emanated from the lands where the first recorded acts of the great human drama were played out.... On the one hand, eastern mysticism, on the other, Oriental love of intrigue, framed the systems later on to be transported to the West with results so tremendous and far reaching." (Secret Societies and Subversive Movements, p.3).

Brothers Amini and Habib, in their book Freemasonry, tell us that according to some scholars there are basically three major opinons concerning the origin of Freemasonry: First, that it began when Moses was with his people in the wilderness. Second, that it started with Herod the Second, Jerusalem's governor for the Roman State; Third, Freemasonry is a creation of Modern Times and was founded in Britain in 1717. According to my research, there are at least sixteen theories or opinions of the origin of Freemasonry, namely, it derived (1) from Adam, (2) from the Ancient Mystery Systems of Egypt, (3) from the mysteries of the ancient Greek and Roman sunworshippers, (4) from the Crusaders, (5) from the Knights Templars, (6) from the Patriarchs,

(7) from the Construction of Solomon's Temple, (8) from the Roman Collegia of Artifices, (9) from Operative Masonry, (10) from Oliver Cromwell, (11) from Rosicrucians, (12) from the Stuarts, (13) from Christopher Wren, at the building of St. Paul's (14) from Dr. Desaguliers, (15) from the Celtic Druids, (16) from the soul of man.

Turning again to the East, we find that there were certain secret societies that sprung up after the death of our Holy Prophet Muhammad (PBUH). Many of these secret organizations were formed by Muslims who believed that there is a deeper and higher meaning to the Holy Qur'an than can be readily seen by the common believer. Others were formed for military and warfare. History tells us that shortly after the Prophet died (PBUH), the enemies of Al-Islam, who had infiltrated the ranks of the Muslims, instigated and created division among the ranks of the believers. Their seeming success led to the death of Umar, Uthman and Ali, Abu Bakr being the only Khalifah to escape their vicious plots. The pre-planned murder of Uthman led to a bloody conflict between Ali, the fourth Khalifah of Islam, and his followers, and Aisha, the wife of the Prophet, and her followers. This conflict became known as the "Battle of the Camel." Fakir Syed Waheed-ud-din reports, "The battle settled no issue and the situation in Hejaz became so disturbed that Ali had to move his headquarters to Iraq. More bloodshed was in store for Ali and another fierce battle was fought at Siffin when the armies of Ali and Mu'awiya clashed...Muslim power was divided into two governments, the government of Mu'awiya in Syria, and that of Ali in the rest of the Islamic domain." Ali was murdered while he was praying in the masjid. He was stabbed with a poisoned sword.

We also learn that the once unified Muslim community of Prophet Muhammad (PBUH) divided into two major groups, differing mainly over the successors of the Prophet. The Shi-ites (as they became known as) claimed the Khalifat (Successors) for the descendants of Prophet Muhammad through Ali, the Prophet's cousin—being indifferent to the majority acceptance of the elected Khalifahs, Abu Bakr, Umar, Uthman and Ali. It should be noted that aside from the division over the line of succession to the Prophet, the Shi-ites did not deviate from the basic principles or pillars of the religion. This point is important to realize because later various secret organizations were formed from the Shi-ites, some of which deviated greatly from the pure teachings of Al-Islam. Some of the groups that formed under the Shi-ites line was (1) The Ismailis, (2) The Qarmatians, (3) The Fatimids, (4) The Druzes, (5) The Assassins, and others. Each of these groups developed their own secrets and methods of imparting them to their members. Some of these groups became well known for their military tactics and operations, while others became known for their learning and high regard for the widom of the Qur'an.

During the period of the Crusades, many of the ideas and practices of these Muslim groups were adopted by the European Christian warriors. More specifically, it was through the Knight Templars that most of the Eastern secret societies' methods were introduced into Europe. The Templars were influenced by the Order of the Assassins. According to the book, Secret Societies Unveiled, "The Order of the Assassins came into our story because the Knights Templars, who introduced Eastern secret society methods into Europe, came into intimate contact with them."

THE MASONIC STRUCTURE

After looking briefly at the history of Freemasonry, let us turn our focus now to the structure or the form of the Masonic System.

SIGNIFICANCE OF THE FIRST THREE DEGREES

Originally the Masonic system consisted of only three degrees; namely the Entered Apprentice, the Fellow Craft, and the Master Mason. Even today they are considered the foundation of Masonry. In fact, all Masons must first receive these degrees before they can ascend up to the higher degrees. The term "Blue Lodge" is used to refer to those three basic degrees.

According to Masonic teachings, these three degrees (Entered Apprentice, Fellow Craft, and Master Mason) allude to the three stage development of the human being: physical, mental and spiritual. Steinmetz explains that not only are the three degrees symbolic of the three stages of human development, but "all of Masonry is contained within the first three degrees." He further points out that the first three degrees "teach that man is made in the image and likeness of his Creator; that he (man) is a triune being composed of body, soul and spirit. Their object is to develop the spiritual side of man's nature, to instruct the candidate how, through the use of mind, to subdue and discipline the physical nature, that the spiritual may predominate." (The Royal Arch, Its Hidden Meaning, p. 8). On page 66 he adds: "In the Entered Apprentice degree, which is the material degree of Freemasonry, the method of experimentation is encountered. Passed to the degree of Fellow Craft, the candidate finds himself on the mental plane. His method of progression is that of observation and he is therein first given philosophic instruction. As a Master Mason, he is introduced to the spiritual."

Albert Pike, although explaining it somewhat differently, arrives at the same conclusion. He writes, "For the

Apprentice, the points of the compass are beneath the square. for the Fellow-Craft, one is above and one beneath. For the Master, both are dominant, and have rule, control and empire over the symbol of the earthly and the material.

Another Masonic writer says that the first three degrees actually represent the Doer, the Knower, and the Thinker, which he claims are three aspects of the human being. This author argues that man is a "triune" being. He explains, "Intelligent matter, that is the Triune Self, is divided into three degrees: those of Apprentice, Fellow Craft and Master... The degree of Master Mason represents the Apprentice and Fellow Craft raised to the degree of Master. As the Apprentice is the Doer, and the Fellow Craft is the Thinker, so, the Master Mason is the Knower. Going through each degree as an individual symbolizes the development of the Apprentice (or Doer) passing to the Fellow Craft (or relation to the Thinker) and being raised to the degree of Master Mason or attaining to relation of the Knower. (Masonry and its Symbols, p. 22, 24).

Technically speaking, the Entered Apprentice degree represents the "ground floor" of King Solomon's Temple; Fellow Craft represents the "Middle Chamber"; and Master Mason is symbolic of the "Sanctum Sanctorum" or the Holy of Holies. These degrees also allude to the physical hunger, the rational search, and the spiritual appetites in the human being; and in the three stage resurrection of Hiram Abiff who, masonically, was murdered by three Jews; Jubela, Jubalo and Jubelum. (Each Mason must re-inact the drama of Hiram Abiff. The term "raised" is specifically applied to this ceremony).

The number three, as a developmental process, is not only important in Masonry, but it is also important in government, religion and metaphysics. The human being has a physical hunger for physical or material things. We also have a desire for knowledge and rational understanding. The mind of man wants answers, it seeks to know its environment. Lastly, the spiritual appetite seeks to know God and the higher wisdom and purpose of man and the creation. In Masonry, these stages are classified as Youth, Manhood, and Age; they are also represented by: the rough ashlar, the perfect ashlar, and the trestle board. In the United States, there are three levels of government: Federal, State, and Local. Each of these levels of government consists of an Executive Branch, a Legislative Branch, and a Judicial Branch. These branches were created to maintain an equilibrium of the power and authority, or "Checks and Balances."

In Genesis we read of Adam, Eve and the Serpent in the Garden of Eden. According to the Bible, one of the powers outwitted the other two. The Serpent manipulates Adam through Eve. Let us hope this does not happen to our government.

In Christianity, and the Bible, we find that three occurs many times. In most cases, it pertains to the same thing as it does in Freemasonry, but most Christians probably do not know it. For example, the baptism is symbolic of cleaning the person physically, mentally and spiritually. The Trinitarian doctrine actually represents the three stages of human growth and development; God the Father, Son and Holy Ghost is just a corruption of the idea of the "triune man." God the Father, it can be said, represents the dominating will to submit to the Creator. The Son represents the state of mind or conscience that is formed after the will is manifested. And lastly, the Holy Ghost can allude to the spirit that dominates the human being. Some people have good spirits and some have bad spirits.

The first three degrees of Freemasonry carry basically the same message. According to the Old Testament, God addressed Samuel in his three stages of development. It tells us that after the third calling, Samuel came to life and realized that God was calling him. According to the story, he went to Eli the Priest. (I Samuel 3:4-9). The number three also appears in the story of Balaam and the Ass. The Bible says the donkey said to Balaam, **"What have I done unto thee, that thou has smitten me these three times?"** (Numers 22:22-32). In the first Book of Kings, we find that

-125-

Elijah raised the Widow's son from the dead by pressing him three times. It reads, **"And he (Elijah) stretched himself upon the child three times."** (17:21-24). Jesus raised the widow's son in the same manner (Luke 7:11). It is also reported that Jesus said concerning the human temple, the spiritual kingdom within **"Destroy this temple, and in three days I will raise it up."** (John 2:19). Jesus Himself, according to Christian dogma rose from the grave on the third day.

Freemasonry, which to a great extent is a progressive science, attempts to teach its members the movement, growth and development of man in his three stages of existence. It stresses through the use of symbols, instructions and initiations, the concept of self mastery. Imam Warith Deen Muhammad, a profound leader, teacher and a student of the Holy Qur'an, expounded heavily on the significance of three stage development. Those who have studied him from 1975 to today, understand and can relate to the symbolic teachings of Freemasonry concerning the three stage development of man. Let us briefly review some of the things he has taught in the early years of his leadership. In a more recent lecture concerning his early teachings, Imam Muhammad said, "Go back and study the articles in which I was talking about three stage development, it lasted for about three years. Then I began to tone down that kind of theory." (New York, March 3, 1983). In his book, As The Light Shineth From the East, we read, "The three sons of Noah are not really flesh and blood sons. They represent the three kinds of motivation that the human being can come into that dominate and give form to his whole life. He evolves up through three levels of motivation. The first is hunger for physical things... secondly, he is motivated to seek knowledge; and thirdly, his spiritual aspiration evolves." (p. 52).

In an article entitled, "Womb of Law, Part 2", he wrote, "Out of the womb (body) of law the human being grows into the womb (body) of moral rationale. We come to that womb and grow still further into the womb (body) of truth. The womb of Truth is the final body that God wants us to take form in and to grow in" (Lectures of Imam Muhammad,

p. 101). Concerning the growth from darkness into light, the Imam explained in a book, "Teachings of W.D. Muhammad": "The human being begins his life in triple darkness: there are three wombs of darkness to grow out of. The growth out of these wombs comes naturally...".

The Bible tells us that Jesus' parents were looking for him for three days, and when they found him, he was in the temple "sitting in the midst of the doctors, both hearing them, and asking them questions." (St. Luke 2:46-50). Imam W.D. Muhammad explained that, "During the three days that Jesus' father and mother were looking for him, he was in school. The three days here does not represent any time period in the sense of physical time or movement. It is a symbolic term meaning that, he had attended the school of Divine teachings, and that he had been taught the three graduations of Divine knowledge. That is why Jesus after being lost for three days, could go to the Temple of the wise and confound them with the knowledge he had accumulated over a period of the three levels of education he received in the Divine school."

He also pointed out that the three Marys that are mentioned in the New Testament represents the three grades of human development. In his early symbolic teachings, he said that the three Marys of the Bible also represent the three types of society. In a 1975 lecture entitled, "Need for Leadership", he explained that Jesus on the cross is a sign of an oppressed and persecuted people, and that "Mary the Mother of Jesus, and Mary the Sister of Martha, and Mary the Prostitute who was reformed,... this is talking about nothing but the three types of society. Society has leadership on three levels. (1) on the level of the doctors of law—the political leadership; (2) another is in the level of the spiritual people, and (3)... those who do not have any leadership."

As we pointed out earlier, the Bible says, Elijah raised the widow's son by pressing him three times. Imam Muhammad said these three presses represent the science of the human urge in the intellect. In the recent book, Imam W.Deen

-127-

<u>Muhammad Speaks From Harlem, NY</u>, we learn that God has put a progressive urge in man, so that he can grow to his full potential. First man is sensitized through his physical body. That sensitizing finally turns on the light in the rational mind. After that, an intuitive urge comes into him. "That is, he is not satisfied with his reasoning, something is moving him, pressuring him to go on and look deeper, search further. They call it the 'intuitive urge'. Those three urges are the progressive life, the progressive behavior and dimension that God has put into us." (p. 58).

According to the history of Prophet Muhammad (PBUH), the angel Gabriel commanded him to read three times. It was only after the third command was given did our Holy Prophet Muhammad read with the Name of Allah. Also, one of the five daily prayers that Muslims are obligated to perform consists of three <u>rakahs.</u> This prayer is called Salatul-Maghrib (sunset prayer). Symbolically, the offering of the Maghrib prayers after sunset alludes to the need for re-enlightenment mentally, morally and spiritually. "In order to be re-enlightened we must undergo a three stage development." Muslims also know that according to the sunnah of Prophet Muhammad, wudu (ablution) is performed by washing certain parts of our body three times.

In each degree, certain "tools" are given to the candidate to identify which degree he has received in Masonry. For example, in the first degree (Entered Apprentice) the candidate is asked: "What are the working tools of an Entered Apprentice?" Answer: "The twenty-four inch gauge and common gavel." Question: "What are the Masonic uses?" Answer: "The Twenty four inch gauge is an instrument made use of by operative Masons to measure and lay out their work, but we as Free and Accepted Masons are taught to make use of it for the more noble and glorious purpose of dividing our time. It being divided into twenty-four equal parts is emblematical of the twenty-four hours of the day which we are taught to divide into three equal parts, whereby we find eight hours for the service of God and a distressed worthy brother, eight for our usual vocations, and eight for refreshment and sleep.

The common gavel is an instrument made use of by operative Masons to break off the weight and superfluous parts of stones, the better to fit them for the builders' use; but we as Free and Accepted Masons are taught to make use of it for the more noble and glorious purpose of divesting our hearts and consciences of the vices and superfluities of life, thereby fitting our minds as living stones for the spiritual building, that house not made with hands, eternal in the heavens."

In the second degree or Fellow Crafts degree, the Mason is asked, "Are you a Fellow Craft?" Answer: "I am, try me." Question: "How will you be tried?" Answer: "By the square." Question: "why by the square?" Answer: "Because it is an emblem of morality and one of the working tools of a Fellow Craft." Question: "What is a square?" Answer: "An angle of ninety degrees or the fortieth part of a circle." The plumb and the level are also the working tools of a Fellow Craft Mason. It is said that the plumb is an instrument made use of by operative Masons to try perpendiculars; the level to prove horizontals. But for Masons, "The plumb admonishes us to walk uprightly in our several stations before God and man, squaring our actions by the square of virtue, ever remembering that we are traveling upon the level of time to that undiscovered country from whose bounds no traveler returns."

In the third of Master Mason degree, the dialogue is as follows: Question: "After being taught how to wear your apron, how were you then disposed of?" Answer: "I was reconducted to the Worshipful Master in the East who presented me with the working tools of a Master Mason, which are all the implements of Masonry indiscriminately, but more especially the trowel, and taught me its use." Question: "What is its use?" Answer: "The trowel is an instrument made for us by operative Masons to spread the cement which unites the building into one common mass; but we as Free and Accepted Masons are taught to make use of it for the more noble and glorious purpose of spreading the cement of brotherly love and affection. That cement which unites us into one sacred band or society of friends and brothers among whom no contention should ever exist, but that noble contention, or rather emulation of who best can work and best agree." (Ronayne's Handbook of Freemasonry, p. 106-107, 148, 253).

The candidate is also given a lambskin apron (this is called the "Rite of Investiture"). In each degree the apron is worn slightly different. The Entered Apprentice is taught to wear his apron <u>with the bib turned up</u>. "It (the apron) is an emblem of innocence and the badge of a Mason. More ancient than the Golden Fleece or Roman Eagle, more honorable than the Star and Garter, or any other order that can be conferred upon you at this time or at any future period," he is told. The Fellow Craft Mason is instructed to wear his apron <u>with the bib turned down and the left corner turned up in the form of a triangle.</u> The Master Mason wears his apron <u>with the corner turned down in the form of a square.</u>

A lodge of Entered Apprentice consists of at least seven members; Fellow Craft consists of at least five, and Master Mason consists of at least <u>three.</u> So we have 7, 5 and 3, which equal 15. In the Masonic Lodge there is the "Master's Carpet" which has 3, 5 and 7 steps (equaling 15). According to Masonic teachings, the three steps allude to the three degrees (Apprentice, Follow Craft and Master Mason) and the three principle offices of the lodge. Namely, the Worshipful Master, Senior Warden and Junior Warden. The five steps are said to represent the five senses and the five order or architecture, i.e. Tuscan, Doric, Ionic, Corithias and Composite. The seven alludes, Masonically, to the seven liberal arts and sciences which are Grammar, Rhetoric, Logic, Arithmetic, Geometry, Music and Astronomy.

If we take the 3, 5 and 7 a little further and look at the number 15, we can gain even more insight (insha'Allah). Let us bear in mind that the many Masonic scholars agree that there is a deeper meaning or "secret doctrine" that is not revealed to the common Mason. Buck writes, "For the greater part, modern Masons are dealing with symbols, the key for the real interpretation of which they never possessed, or even suspected that it existed." (Mystic Masonry, p. 30). In fact, Albert Pike says to the candidate: "Imagine not that you will become indeed a Mason by learning what is commonly called the "work," or even by becoming familiar with our tradition. Masonry has a history, a literature, a philosophy. Its allegories and traditions will teach you much, but much is to be sought elsewhere." (Morals and Dogma, p. 107). In the first degrees, as mentioned eariler, symbolically the Masons evolve physically, mentally and spiritually. The number 15 can be connected to this progression or development. Fifteen represents the five senses evolved three times. Albert Pike says, "much is to be sought elsewhere." The fifteenth degree of Scottish Rite Masonry gives us a clue of where further understanding can be secured. The name of the 15th degree is "Knight of the East.[2] Earlier we spoke of the East as being the source of light and understanding, both symbolically and literally (from a historical point of view). According, Buke states, "All writers, however, agree in conclusion that the symbols and traditions of Freemasonry come for the far East, and go back to the remotest antiquity. So that the saying that the Mason journeys from West to East in search of light is literally true." (Mystic Masonry p.140). In the religion of Al-Islam there are five basic pillars that support the faith. Once these pillars are truly carried into practice the Muslims and believers benefit physically, mentally and spiritually. Looking at the fifteenth degree, we find that the "march" or foot sign of Knight of the East is "five long steps."

According to Masonic tradition, there were originally fifteen craftsmen who plotted to kill the Master Builder. The legend says he was struck three times. It can be reasoned then that they wanted to kill him physically or morally, mentally and spiritually. His five senses were taken away on all three levels. In the tenth degree called, "Master Elect of Fifteen", the lodge is lit with 15 lights. It is in this degree that the three murderers of Hiram Abiff are illustrated in their deathly form. According to the ritual, "In the East is a skeleton representing Jubelum; in the West, one representing Jubela; and in the South, one representing Jubelo on whose blood the flies have sucked." These figures are said to represent first, ignorance or darkness; second, superstition or error; and third, egotism or ambition. The fifteenth degree tells us then, that if man's five senses died in all three levels, then he must be raised or enlightened again on all three levels. The Elect of Fifteen represent that a victory over the forces of darkness or ignorance. This is why fifteen lights burn in the lodge in this degree.

Masonic tradition says that Hiram Abiff, the widow's son, laid in the grave 15 days. In the Masonic ceremony of raising it is said, "Most Excellent King Solomon, owing to the high state of putrefaction, the body having been dead already fifteen days, the skin slips and it cannot be so raised." (See Duncan's Ritual of Freemasonry, and Tonaynes's Handbook of Freemasonry). In Masonic catechism, the questions are asked concerning the "raising." Question: "From what to what, by what, on what?" Answer: "From a dead level to a living perpendicular to the square, by the lions paw, on the _five_ points of fellowship. The five points of fellowship are symbolic of the five senses. In order to raise the intellect of the human being, you must first appeal to his physical senses. If the five senses are not alive, then no information from the outside would be received within.

Imam W. D. Muhammad explained the meaning and importance of fifteen as alluding to the three stages of man's growth, on August 8, 1983 at Malcolm Shabazz Masjid in Harlem, New York. He said, "The most important idea for Muslims is oneness (Tauheed), Allah is One.... Let us look at the five manifests on a higher level. We have talked about five in the flesh or sensory body, five in the mind. Now, five should go another distance. We will be able to articulate, we will have insight, we will be able to see. And the angel pressed the Prophet three times. He (the Prophet) sensed it, "I don't read." He reflected on it, "I can't read." Then something else happened and he began to read. What is that? Purpose. Purpose. Man does not just want to see and respond. Man does not want to just see and reflect. Man wants to know what is the purpose. Man wants to see into matter, not just on matter. So when we are able to see into things and understand their natural workings, understand their purpose in the universe, or in the universal order of things, we are men of science. And when we know the purpose of a thing, then we are home.... How many plates get you to home base? Three! First, second, third, home. Right? You have to go over three to get home...Once you get off three, you are home. What does off three mean? Free of three. How are you free of three? When you know how to use that knowledge as God intended it to be used. Then that knowledge is not mastering you, you are free of the mystery or the weight of that knowledge... Man is a thinking creature. He reflects, but once he gets insight, that is home. Insight will take him home. Because I can use the knowledge of insight to go and correct my life...What is 15? That is five gone three steps. Five took three steps, out of the sensory body, into the reflecting mind (rational mind) out of the rational mind, into the inner workings for knowledge, or insight."

The Master Mason is supposed to be a man of spiritual insight. The first three degrees are designed to prepare the candidate for the further or higher degrees. The manner in which the candidate is prepared for initiation in each degree is also indicative of the material, mental and spiritual. The Entered Apprentice is prepared for initiation by first having the left leg of his pants rolled above the knee, so as to make his left foot, leg and knee naked. The left sleeve of his shirt is rolled back above the elbow. The left breast of his shirt is tucked back, leaving his left breast bare. A slipper is put over his right foot, a hoodwink is put over his eyes, and a rope (called a cable-tow) is tied once around his neck. In the second degree, or Fellow Craft degree, he is prepared on the opposite side, the rope is tied twice around his naked right arm, just above the elbow.

The Master Mason is prepared as follows: Both pants legs are turned up above the knees, both sleeves of his shirt are rolled back above the elbows. The shirt in most cases is taken completely off. A blindfold is put over his eyes. The rope is now tied three times around his waist. And there he stands barefooted duly and truly prepared, ready to be initiated into the secret mysteries of Masonry. Harold W. Percival in his book Masonry and Its Symbols explains the meaning of the "preparation for initiation" as follows: "He (the candidate) is there divested of his clothing. That ceremony stands for the removal of the things that hold him to the outer world, such as possessions and indications of station and rank. It means that he is separated from the past, so that he can enter on a new course... A hoodwink or blindfold is put over his eyes, so that he feels he is in darkness, without light and cannot find his way. Then the thing he most desires is light... The cabletow stands for the umbilical cord by which all bodies are prepared for birth. it stands for the senses of sight, hearing, taste and smell by which the candidate (the conscious self in the body) is held after birth, which bind him to nature and lead him in darkness. It stands for Masonry which brings him out of the physical world of darkness into the light... The cabletow also is the line on the breath-from that binds one to Masonry, to destiny, to rebirth and re-existence."

After the candidate is taken through the initiation ceremonies, he is led to the altar where he takes the oath of secrecy. For each degree, the oath is slightly different and the manner in which it is taken is also different. The Entered Apprentice is made to kneel on his naked left knee, his right leg forming a square, his left hand holding the Bible. Square and Compass is called the "Three Great Lights" in Masonry. The candidate is able to see the three great lights by the assistance of three lesser lights. The three lesser lights are three candles that are placed in a triangular form around the altar. Masonically, they represent the sun, moon and Master of the Lodge. The so-called Worshipful Master explains to the candidate that "The Bible is given as the rule and guide of our faith; the Square, to square our actions; and the Compass to circumscribe and keep us within due bounds." Many Masons and Christians have asked, "Is the Bible superior to the Square and Compass or visa versa?"

-134-

If it is superior, why is it beneath the square and compass on the altar?" If it is superior, why is it beneath the square and compass on the altar?" The answer that is generally given is that the Bible is the foundation of Masonry and that the Bible gives insight into the wisdom of the square and compass. Others argue that the square and compass are above the Bible because the Bible was/is sealed, and that the key to unlocking the mysteries of the Bible is in understanding the meaning of the square and compass. Most Masonic writers agree that the square is a symbol of the physical and the compass is a symbol representing the spiritual; and that once a person has knowledge of the physical and the spiritual, he can break the secret code language in the Bible.

THE PROGRESSION OF THE COMPASS AND THE SQUARE

In the first degree, both points of the compass are under the square. The candidate, after being brought to "light" is told that the square is above the compass because he (the candidate) has not yet progressed to the point where he can control his passions. Percival writes, "...the points of the square are above the compass, that is to say, his (the candidate or initiate) feelings and desires are not controlled by his Rightness and Reason, and that the third light, the square, is dark; that is, the light does not not reach his feelings and desire." (p.10) Steinmetz tells us that both the compass and the square are symbolic of man: the Square, the material man; the compass, the spiritual man. "And, as the square is placed above the compass, we are to understand that in this degree (Entered Apprentice or First Degree) the material dominates the spiritual."

In the Second degree (Fellow Craft) the right point of the compass is raised above the left point of the square. The Ritual states, "one point of the compass is elevated above the square which is to teach you that you have as yet received light in Masonry but partially." Percival explains, "In being brought to light in this degree, he perceives one point of the compass above the square, symbolic of the fact that he receives light through the rightness of his thinker and that he will be guided in his actions from that point, that light." (p. 18). The position of the compass and the square, in this degree, represents the dawning of conscience and mental enlightenment, which according to some Masonic scholars is the next step after the material and the step before spiritual understanding.

In the third degree (Master Mason's degree) both points of the compass are raised above the points of the square. This is the point of "illumination". The Worshipful Master says to the candidate: "My brother, upon being brought to light in this degree, you discover the three great lights in Masonry, as before, with this difference, both points of the compass elevated above the square, which is to teach you never to lose sight of the Masonic application of that useful and valuable instrument which teaches friendship, morality and brotherly love."

Buck gives us a deeper interpretation. He writes, "The Square with its one right angle and its scale of measurements applies to surfaces and solids, and deals with the apparently fixed states of matter. It represents solidarity, symmetry and proportion; and this involves the sciences of arithmetic and geometry. The Compass with movable angle set in the Lodge at an angle of sixty degrees, applies to the circle and the sphere; to movements and revolutions... In the Lodge the square and compass cross each other, and this fact is made a symbol of progression, from the degree of Entered Apprentice to that of Master. The compass is set at an angle of sixty degrees and is representative of the movements of spirit, and, if crossed at a certain distance from the angle, will produce an equilateral triangle; the three angles and the three sides equal, it now represents perfect equilibrium or proportion." (p.130).

According to other Masonic writers, the union of the compass and the square represents the union of the masculine and feminine principles that are necessary for the procreation of life. Maguer writes, "The relative positions of the square and compass in the first three degrees, namely that of the Entered Apprentice, the Fellow Craft and the Master Mason, signify the gradual ascending of the spirit, the masculine principle over matter, the feminine principle; that is of the masculine principle building out of the material substance of woman, a Mason, a temple fit for the in-dwelling of an immortal spirit." (p. 390). Beroge states, "The Square and the Compass represent the union of the Old and New Testaments." On page 841 of his book, Morals and Dogma, Albert Pike tells us that, "For the Master, the Compass of Faith is above the Square of Reason, but both rest upon the Holy Scripture and combine to form the Blazing Star of Truth."

Let us look at this progression from another point of view. The compass and square as an emblem or ring usually has the letter "G" in the center. According to Masonic teachings, the letter "G" is an initial representing God, Geometry and Gnosis (Gnosis is the science of understanding esoteric or spiritual truths). As already pointed out, the movements of the compass and the square represents the progression of human growth and development. If we examine the meaning of the letter "G", the same message is revealed, except with far more implications. The word "God" is really not accepted by Muslims as a good word for the Creator. The word "GOD" reversed spells "DOG". It should be rejected as a term referring to the Creator, Allah. The word "God" really refers to a principle for advancing man from a low state (dog) to a higher state (god, ruler), just as the progression of the compass and the square does. The Holy Qur'an says Allah created man in the best mold, but man can be reduced to the lowest of low. (95:4-6). The evil-minded ones who learn the science of human nature, use this knowlede to manipulate the human being.

Let us look further. The compass and the square are really two triangles---one pointing upright and the other pointing down. In Masonry, the three sided triangle represents the three dimensional nature of man: physical, mental and spiritual. The manipulators take the knowledge of human growth and reverse it so that the human being will always be on a low level looking up to the manipulators for light and understanding. In the higher degrees of Masonry, the triangle is referred to as the "Pyramid". As we will point out later, the pyramid, among other things, represents the science for manipulating human behavior.

Concerning the use and meaning of the word God, Imam Warith Deen Muhammad explained in a lecture entitled, "Pharoah and Egypt" (March 21, 1982) that this term (God) was not formed to apply to the real God, Allah. This term applies to a behavior in nature, and that behavior is given to us in the Qur'an where it says He created man in the most excellent mold. But by consequence of his (man's) own disbelief, his own ignorance, he is reduced to the lowest of the low.... This term has nothing to do with the characteristics or attributes of God at all. Another proof of that is this: the god that they introduce to the world for our eyes to see and identify with is not a spirit, it is a man. A man they call Jesus! (May Allah save the Prophet from these bad lies that they tell on him.) So we see now that we are talking about a behavioral nature, and not an attribute of God. Now, can't you see how it is so easy for a world of religious people to accept that this name be abused---"Goddamn, etc." A popular magazine came out with a headline around 1957 or 1958, "God Is Dead." They don't care, because with them that God means something else, not the real God. They say they got a name for God they can't pronounce. It is secret, they are forbidden to pronounce it. They give it in four letters and it has fourteen letters. Four characters from Hebrew. But when they tell you what it is in English, the number of letters they use is fourteen. They call it the "Tetragrammaton".... if this word means not the Almighty Allah, but a behavioral principle in man and nature, it says this: That principle has the possibilities of taking man to the highest, furthest reach in excellence, and for them that furtherest reach is God. Alright, but it also has a possibility of allowing man to regress to the lowest possible ebb. The lowest possible ebb is dog...

"A mind or a combination of minds that would conceive of man as having the potential to go to a point of excellence where they say he is the same as God (the Creator), is diabolical, satanic, wicked, it is the devil. Scripture, the Bible, points that kind of mentality out as the mentality of the devil. It says Satan conspired to exalt himself up even to the position of the Most High God"... And what does Allah pronounce? He pronounces a sentence on such persons, and He says, **"Oh you, ascend to the highest heights, I will bring you down to the lowest of the low"**. So they have that kind of terminology in this name, in this spelling. What does that suggest too? It suggests further a science for ruling man and society. If they know the nature of man, his aspirations, and his natural motivations, then they can exploit him, they can influence his behavior over his eyes and over his head, and they can drop him down to the dog pen whenever they get ready. And they can urge him, stimulate him to go up the ladder to excellence, if they want to."

In Freemasonry, they claim that man can somehow become or progress mentally to the point where he himself becomes God. Let us look for a moment at some key points.

First, the leader of the Lodge is called Worshipful Master. Just think of a man being called **worshipful**. Jesus said, **"there is none worthy of worship but the Master (the Creator)"**. Does not the word worship suggest that one submits to the Creator. Webster defines worship as follows: To honor or reverence as a divine being or supernatural power.

Second, the Scottish Rite Order of Fremasonry, the most powerful Masonic Rite in the world, consists of thirty-three degrees. The reason why it consists of thirty-three degrees, according to noted Masonic scholars, is because it is generally believed that Jesus lived only thirty-two or thirty-three years. Jesus is believed to be God by much of Christian society. What is the subtle message? The subtle message is that once man ascends up the Masonic ladder he becomes as God. It is called the "Christ consciousness".

In the thirty-second degree, the message is more direct. The candidate is told that he has now learned all that there is to know of God and the mysteries of man. On page 412 of the Scottish Rite Masonry Vol.2, it reads: "You have learned all that ancient and modern philosophy can teach in regard to the great mysteries of God and the universe." Steinmetz, a noted Masonic writer explains that man can actually become a part of the Creator. He alludes to the word atonement as representing that oneness. He suggests that it means "at-one-moment". In his book The Royal Arch, Its Hidden Meaning, he gives a picture of the six pointed star and writes, "The six-pointed star, the shield of David, symbol of the union of God and the Perfect man-at-one-ment." Albert Pike states, "In the heaven of human conceptions, it is humanity that creates God; and men think that God

-140-

has made them in His image because they make Him in their's." (p. 736). He further states, "...for do what you will, the highest efforts of human thought can conceive nothing higher than the supremacy of intellect; and so he ever comes back to some familiar type of exalted humanity."

This idea of man becoming God is not a new invention. Scripture tells us that Pharoah claimed he **was** God. Also, those who are familiar with the old teachings of the Nation of Islam in America, know that its founder, Fard Muhammad, claimed that he was God, and that man evolves to the point where he becomes God. On page 6 of the book <u>Message To The Blackman</u> it reads, "God is a man and we just cannot make Him other than man, lest we make Him an inferior one; for man's intelligence has no equal in other than man. His wisdom is infinite; capable of accomplishing anything that his brain can conceive." This diabolical message is found throughout Masonry.

Allah says in the Qur'an that He created man and provided him with faculties and the signs (creation) so that he can develop his mind. (16:74, 76-77). The Qur'an also states, "**It is we who have placed you with authority on earth, and provided you therein with means for the fulfillment of your life: Small are the thanks that ye give!**" (7:10).

WORDS, TOKENS, AND SIGNS

In the First Degree, the candidate is instructed to step off on his left foot. In the Second Degree he steps off on his right foot. And the Master Mason is to step off with his left foot. The Master Mason brings the heels of his feet together forming a square. The ritual states that Senior Deacon says, "Brother Senior Warden, it is the order of the Worshipful Master that you teach the candidate to approach the East by one upright regular step, his feet forming the angle of a square, his body erect, at the alter before the Worshipful Master." The Senior Deacon then instructs the candidate as follows; "Mr. _____, you will step off one step with your left foot, bring the heel of the right to the hollow of the left, forming the angle of a square." In the Second Degree, he says, "You will now step off one step with your right foot, bringing the heel of the left to the hollow of the right." In the Third Degree (Master Mason) he says, "You will now take one advance step with your left foot, and bring the heel of your right foot to the heel of the left, your feet forming the angle of a square." (pg. 67, 120, 169).

The candidate is told that the passwords are Boaz, Joachin, Shibboleth and Tubal-cain. He is also given what is called the sacred word, which is really a substitute word Mah-hah-bone. This is called the "Rite of Instructions."

The candidate is taught that the form of a Lodge is an oblong rectangle extending from east to west between north and south, "forming the earth, heavens and from the surface to the center." The Supports or pillars of Masonry are metaphorically called "Wisdom, Stength and Beauty". According to the Masonic ritual a Lodge has six jewels, three immovable and three movable. The immovable jewels are the Square, Level and Plumb. The movable jewels are the rough ashler, perfect ashler and trestle-board.

Masonic philosophy teaches that symbolically the four points of entrance are: Temperance, Fortitude, Prudence and Justice. Its tenets are said to be "Brotherly Love, Relief and Truth." Percival, in his book Masonry and Its Symbols, explains, "The points of entrance and the six jewels are quite interesting. He writes, "The perfect points of the Apprentices' Entrance are four. They are the four cardinal virtues: temperance is habitual self-restraint or control of one's passionate impulses and appetites; fortitude means constraint, courage, patience and endurance without fear of danger; prudence means skill in right thinking and in the performance of right action; and justice is knowledge of the rights of oneself and others, and in thinking and acting in accordance with that knowledge."

"The candidate learns about the jewels. There are six jewels, three movable: the rough ashler, the perfect ashler and the trestle board. The rough ashler is the symbol of the present, imperfect physical body; the perfect ashler is the symbol of the physical body after it has been perfected; the trestle-board, the symbol of the breath-form, on which the designs of the building are drawn. These three jewels are called movable because they perish after each life or are carried from life to life. The   jewels are the square, the level, and the plumb. The square symbolizes desire; the level feeling; and the plumb the pattern of the perfect body which is on the breath form. These three are called immovable, because they are of the Triune Self and do not die." (p. 14-15).

ASCENDING UP THE MASONIC PYRAMID

After the candidate has learned all of the lessons he is required to learn in the "Blue Lodge" (First three degrees), and has become a Master, he may now choose to ascend up further into the Masonic system. He has the option of either being initiated into the Scottish Rite system of thirty-three degrees (inclusive of the first three degrees) or the York Rite which consists of seven degrees. In many cases, Masons join both Rites. The title of the degrees are listed as follows:

Degree	Scottish Rite	York Rite
33rd	Sovereign Grand Inspector General	Order of Knights Templar
32nd	Sublime Prince of The Royal Secret *	
31st	Grand Inspect Inquisitor Commander	
30th	Grand Elect Knight Kodash	
29th	Knight of Andrew	
28th	Knight of the Sun of Prince Adept	
27th	Knight Commander of The Temple	Order of Knights of Malta
26th	Prince of Mercy	
25th	Knight of the Brazen Serpent	

24th	Prince of the Tabernacle	Order of Red Cross
23rd	Chief of the Tabernacle	
22nd	Prince of Libanus or Knight of the Royal Axe	
21st	Patriarch Noachite	
20th	Master Ad Vitam or Master of All Symbolic Lodges	
19th	Grand Pontiff	
18th	Knight of Rose Croix of H.R.D.M.	Royal Arch Mason
17th	Knight of the East and West	
16th	Prince of Jerusalem	
15th	Knight of the East or Sword	Most Excellent Master
14th	Grand Elect Mason	
13th	Master of the Ninth Arch or Royal Arch of Solomon	
12th	Grand Master Architect	Past Master
11th	Sublime Master Elected or Elu of the Twelve	
10th	Master Elect of Fifteen	
9th	Master Elect of Nine	

8th	Intendent of the Building	
7th	Provost and Judge	
6th	Intimate Secretary	
5th	Perfect Master	Mark Master
4th	Secret Master	
3rd	Master Mason	
2nd	Fellow Craft	
1st	Entered Apprentice	

*Shriners Degree

Both Rites, though distinct, actually work together as one system. C. H. Stauffacher, D.D., LL.D., 33rd Degree and Charles P. Roney, D.D. in their Introduction to Freemasonry and the Holy Bible, write, "The 'York Rite' and the 'Scottish Rite' are distinct systems, but they work harmoniously together, and may be regarded in a general sense as a single fraternity. Membership in the Blue Lodge is necessary for advancement in both of these systems." (p.9)

MASONIC ASCENSION

It is said that Masonry is a "universal brotherhood" that includes Muslims, Christians and Jews. Through its methods of initiation and instructions, it attempts to teach its members stage by stage and degree by degree. Amini and Habib in their book Freemasonry point out that "Human beings live in the temple, and are fed the principles of freemasonry; its values are inculcated for a specified period of time. When he becomes worthy of advancement he ascends, by degrees, until he reaches the thirty-third, at which time he becomes a Temple Custodian." (p. 17).

The Holy Qur'an tells us that Allah raises the human being stage by stage, and that He is the one who brings us from darkness into light. He says, **"Wherewith Allah guideth all who seek His good pleasure to ways of peace and safety, and leadeth them out of darkness, by His will, unto the light, guideth them to a path that is straight."** (H.Q. 5:18).

The Masonic claim of universality is based primarily on the fact that it (as an institution and a philosophy) incorporates the ideologies and philosophies of the world. Therefore, for example, a Christian will see something in Freemasonry that he can relate to, so also will a Muslim, Jew, etc. The problem with this is that, for example, if a Muslim for some strange reason joins the Masonic institution and ascends up to the thirty-third degree, not only would he have taken oaths that are un-Islamic, but he would have somewhere along the way pretended to be a Christian knight or Jewish vanguard. This would be hypocritical. Prophet Muhammad (PBUH) said, "The worst amongst the people is the double-faced one; he comes to some people with one face and to others with the other face." (Sahih Muslim).

If we look at all the degrees in Masonry, we can see that it is an elaborate system of views and philosophies. The Bible tells us that the "Tower of Babel" was the same way. It tells us that there were so many languages (i.e., various philosophies and ideologies) in one system until the people became confused and just started babbling at the mouth. As we pointed out before, one of the subtle messages in Masonry is that man can become so wise that he becomes God. He reaches heaven. Does not the Bible say the Tower of Babel was built with the intent of reaching heaven. It (Bible) states and **"they said, "Go to, let us build us a city, and a tower, whose top may reach unto heaven** (Genesis 11:14). Abd Al-Qadir, a Sufi, points out that in Masonry the message is "that man himself is divine and is the architect

-147-

of his own greatness. Thus the Temple is his design for the enthronement of human power and domination. (Resurgent Islam, 1400 Hijra p. 19).

As mentioned earlier, a lot can be learned from the study of Freemasonry, but even much more can be learned from the study of the Holy Qur'an and the Sunnah of Prophet Muhammad (PBUH). In fact, most of the precious wisdom and pure truths that exist in Freemasonry and other esoteric schools of wisdom is taken from the Qur'an and the religion of Al-Islam. Imam W. Deen Muhammad profoundly pointed out how Allah commands the Muslims to ascend up into the wisdom of Qur'an and earnestly seek to understand it (47:24). He said, (lecture 3/6/83, New York), "...you are in the world trying to climb up their mountains of knowledge, and you are missing the real one that can really liberate you. How come you won't climb up the Qur'an? That is what Allah is saying here ((47:24). Then the challenge is put to them: It (Qur'an) says, 'if it wasn't from the God Almighty, they would have already found in it many contradictions.' Because you know the enemies of this world pick things apart. They get a team of scientists from around the world, and they will come at you with everything they have. But the challenge was put to. them fourteen hundred years ago: If you can match these verses with wisdom, produce one like it, if you can! (2:23) And they have not been able to do it yet. Instead, their learned men have snatched a page of the Qur'an, ran with it in the closet and called their other learned men in the closet to use their lights to search it. Then they come up with secret schools and make people pay money to come in and get a piece of the stolen wisdom."

SYMBOLIC REFERENCE TO THE ASCENSION
OF JESUS AND MUHAMMAD

The thirty-three degrees of the Scottish Rite Order of Freemasonry actually alludes to the thirty three years of Jesus' life. But more importantly it alludes to the belief that at thirty-three he ascended to heaven. The Bible says that after Jesus laid three days in the grave (materialism), he ascended up into heaven. The Bible also tells us that Jesus said, "**It is expedient that I go away so that the Comforter can come.**" Nowhere in the Bible do we read that Jesus returned after he ascended to heaven. He wanted the bliss of heaven to be a reality on earth. He prayed, "**Thou kingdom come (on earth) as it is in heaven.**" According to Masonic teachings, the light is at the top of their order, and once a person ascends up to the top (the thirty-third degree), he receives the pure light of truth which gives him spiritual and mental vision or insight. The proof of this is evident in their symbol of the Pyramid with the eye over it with rays of light. (This symbol is also on the American dollar bill). Once the Mason receives the light (knowledge), he must swear never to bring it down from heaven and share it with the common masses of people. Inspite of the fact that Jesus himself said, "**If a person has a light, let it shine,**" they subtly suggest that Jesus did not share the real light (understanding) of heaven with the masses, because he ascended to heaven and did not return. Furthermore, he said, "**there are many things I can tell you, but you can't bear them now.**"

By the process of independent reasoning and investigation we also find that the thirty three degrees allude to the ascension of the spiritual urge in man, which was typified in Jesus. The spiritual nature in man, alone, is not designed to rule humanity because we are creatures of mind and body. In fact, the Qur'an says, "**If there were settled on earth angels walking about in the peace and quiet, we should certainly have sent them down from the heavens an angel for an apostle**" (17:95). Therefore, Jesus, typifying the spiritual nature in man, had to leave or take a subordinate position so that the Comforter could come.

Both the Bible and the Qur'an say that Jesus was born of the spirit (called the "Ruh" of Allah) of God, which is to tell us that he was predominantly spiritual. He was mostly concerned with the spiritual side of man. This is not to say that he was not rational. No! The Bible shows us that he used rational parables and methods for delivering his message to the people. His characteristic was predominantly spiritual. In fact, most of the Christians who sincerely follow Jesus are known mainly by their spirituality. The Christian community is predominantly a spiritual community. The Scottish Rite Order has as its main symbol the double headed eagle, which is symbolic of the spiritual ascension of man. Wings are a symbol of spiritual development. Technically, according to Masonic authorities, the double headed eagle represents the "Masonic Empire of the East and the West" (Mackey's Revised Encyclopedia of Feemasonry, Vol.1).

On the other side of the Masonic Pyramid, we find that the York Rite Order only consists of seven degrees. The seven degrees also allude to the process of ascension upwards to the light. Seven is a number which represents completion or wholeness. Vera Stanley Adler, in her book The finding of the Third Eye, writes, "The number seven represents the final turning of man inwards to the spiritual life, to the study of sciences and truths, discipline and organization." (p. 114). Imam W. Deen Muhammad states in his latest book that, "seven represents insight into the scientific order of the universe" (p. 52). The Masonic Encyclopedia says, "the word seven signifies full or complete." (p. 693). Symbolically, the ascension of the seven grades or degrees of the York Rite represents the complete ascension of man or the "complete man", the model human being. It does not just represent the spiritual urge in man, rather it represents the ascension or full development of the total man. The complete man or model human being is a man of science, rational discourse, human sentiment and spiritual awareness. He is a **balanced** man.

The seven degrees of the York Rite do not represent the ascension of Jesus or the spiritual urge. It represents the ascension of Prophet Muhammad (PBUH). Remember, in Masonry the candidate ascends up each degree in search of light. The Qur'an tells us that Prophet Muhammad came down with the light. In Al-Islam we learn that the Prophet Muhammad ascended up to the seventh heaven. And on each level he met one of the prophets that preceeded him. According to the Hadith, the angel Gabriel took the prophet Muhammad to each level of heaven and introduced him to the prophet that was on that level. The Hadith tells us that the Prophet Muhammad (PBUH) met Adam, Jesus and John, Joseph, Enoch, Aaron, Moses and Abraham. (Sahih Muslim, p. 102). When the Prophet Muhammad returned, he brought the light down with him. He did not stay up in heaven and just bathe in the precious light of Revelation and salat. No, he returned and shared the light with humanity.

If we look at the Scottish Rite and the York Rite as one system, then we see that there are actually forty degrees. What happens when both Rites are joined together? It forms the Shriners degree. The Shriners organization is a combination of the Scottish Rite and the York Rite. According to the Shriners rituals, only those Masons that have advanced to at least the 32nd degree of the Scottish Rite or those who have advanced to the degree of Knights Templar of the York Rite can earn the Shrine degree. In the Shriners degree, the candidate learns some of the wisdom of Al-Islam. In the Noble's (Shriner's) Quiz Book many questions and answers concerning the religion of Al-Islam are discussed. It reads, "What is the Koran?" Answer: "The Holy Book of Islam." Question: "What does the word **Koran** mean?" Answer: "Discourse." Question: "Who is known as the Prophet of Islam?" Answer: "Mohammed." Question: "What year was the Prophet born?" Answer: "A.D. 570." Question: "Who told the Prophet, in a vision, that there was only one God?" Answer: "The angel Gabriel." Question: "How old was the prophet when he had this vision?" Answer: "Forty." Question: "In what year did the Prophet make his flight to Medina?" Answer: "A.D. 622." Question: "Where are the hot sands located?" Answer: "On the coast of Arabia near the Red Sea." Question: "Why does a Noble (Shriner) have to travel over the hot sands?" Answer: "In order to worship at the Shrine." Question: "Where is the Shrine located?" Answer: "In Mecca". Question: "What venerable object does a noble see at the Shrine?" Answer: "The Black Stone." Question: "Symbolically, what is the form of the Black Stone? What acts of worship are to be performed at the Shrine?" Answer: "Walk around the Sacred Mosque three times and kiss the Black Stone seven times." Question: "Where is the Black Stone kept?" Answer: "In the Kaaba." Question: "Where is the Kaaba located?" Answer: "In the court of the Great Mosque at Mecca." Question: "What does the Arabic greeting 'es selamu aleikum' mean?" Answer: "Peace be with you."

The number **forty**, which is represented by the union of the Scottish Rite degrees and the York Rite degrees, is very important in Masonic symbolism. The noted Masonic Scholar, Albert Mackey, points out in his Encyclopedia that "The alleged period of probation of our first parents in Eden; the continuous deluge of forty days and nights." He also points out that Jesus fasted for forty days, and Moses and Elijah spent forty years in the desert. "Moses was forty days and nights on the mount...the forty days of grace allotted to Nineveh for repentance." He further explains, "The multiple of two perfect numbers—four and ten. This was deemed a sacred number, as commemorating many events of religious significance." (p.364). History also tells us that the Holy Prophet Muhammad received the first revelation of the Qur'an at the age of forty. Albert Pike, one of Masonry's most prominent writers (who also was the Sovereign Grand Commander of the Southern Supreme Council, of the Ancient and Accepted Scottish Rite) says, concerning the success of Prophet Muhammad: "The law of Mahomet (Muhammad) still governs a fourth of the human race; and Turk and Arab, Moor and Persian and Hindu, still obey the Prophet, and pray with their faces turned toward Mecca; and he (Muhammad), and not the living, rules and reigns in the fairest portions of the Orient" (Morals and Dogma, p. 313).

The wise know the power and wisdom of the Qur'an and the religion of Al-Islam. Many of the prominent leaders in America and throughout the world were/are Masons and Shriners. In fact, here in the United States, it has long been believed that in order to become President, you must belong to the Masonic organization. Although our research does not confirm that theory in its entirety, it does reveal that almost half of the total number of presidents beginning with George Washington were Masons. Furthermore, we find that most of those individuals who framed the Constitution and signed the Declaration of Independence were Masons.

PRESIDENTS WHO WERE MASONS

(1) George Washington; (2) Thomas Jefferson; (3) James Madison; (4) James Monroe; (5) Andrew Jackson; (6) James Knox Polk; (7) James Buchanan; (8) Andrew Johnson; (9) James A. Garfield; (10) William McKinely; (11) Theodore Roosevelt; (12) William Howard Taft; (13) Warren G. Harding; (14) Franklin D. Roosevelt; (15) Harry Truman; and, (16) Gerald R. Ford.

Our research has been unable to, at this time, provide evidence that President Jimmy Carter and/or President Ronald Reagan are Masons.

VICE PRESIDENTS WHO WERE MASONS

Our research reveals that the following Vice Presidents were Masons: Schuyler Calfax; Aaron Burr; Daniel Tompkins; J.C. Breckenridge; George Dallas; Charles Fairbanks; Garrett Hobart; Andrew Johnson; Richard Johnson; William King; Thomas Marshall; Theodore Roosevelt; Adlai Stevenson; Henry Wallace and Harry Truman.

MASONS WHO SIGNED THE DECLARATION OF INDEPENDENCE

Masonic authorities boast that the great majority of the fifty-six signers of the American Declaration of Independence were Masons. H.L. Haywood in his book <u>Famous Masons and Masonic Presidents</u> explains that most of the records on the fifty-six signers have been lost. "But it is of certainty that: John Hancock, Lyman Hall, Benjamin Franklin, Joseph Hernes, William Hooper, Thomas Nelson,Jr., Thomas McKean, Robert Treat Paine, John Penn, Richard Stockton, Roger Sherman, Matthew Thornton, William Whipple, George Walton, and John Witherspoon (were Masons).

OTHER PROMINENT MASONS

Whalen points out some of the other prominent individuals who have entered the "Masonic Door." To mention just a few: Paul Revere, Alexander Hamilton, Patrick Henry, Lafayette, John Jacob Astor, Mark Twain, Henry Ford, Will Rogers, General Pershing, Henry Clay, John Philip Sousa, Bolivar, Sam Houston, Irving Berlin, Charles Lindbergh, Albert Pike, John T. Desaguliers, Andrew Michael Ramsey, Albert G. Mackey, Mozart, Kit Carson, Frederick The Great, Napoleon, Adam Weishaupt, J. Edgar Hoover, Benedict Arnold and Aaron Burr.

PROMINANT SHRINERS

Senator Barry Goldwater, Franklin Roosevelt, Thomas E. Dewey, Irving Berlin, Harold Lloyd, Chief Justice Earl Warren, Astronauts Gordon and Cooper and Virgil Grissom, Arthur Godfrey, Gene Autry, Red Skelton.

*(NOTE: The information contained in this section was compiled from four main sources: (1) Masonic Bible, Introduction; (2) famous Masons and Masonic Presidents, 1968; (3) The Shriners, by William J. Whalen, 1966, and (4) Christianity and American Freemasonry, 1958.)

MASONIC RACISM

Before briefly discussing this subject, it is imperative that the following question be asked. What would make the African-American Mason think that the Caucasian Masons would share with them their wisdom and secrets? The Caucasians have not even shown genuine respect for African-Americans as human beings over the last few centuries, not to mention the inhumane treatment that they issued out to our foreparents. History tells us that a Black man named Prince Hall and thirteen other Blacks were made Freemasons in a military lodge in Boston on March 6, 1775. Prince Hall then applied to the Grand Lodge of England for a charter, which he received on September 29, 1784. The first name of the lodge he established was "African Lodge No.459." Albert G. Mackey explains that, "This lodge had little connection with the Grand Lodge of England for many years, and its registration...was stricken from the rolls of the United Grand Lodge of England when new lists were made in 1813." It should be noted that Prince Hall tried diligently, though unsuccessfully, to obtain recognition from the American Masonic lodges, before he petitioned the 'Mother Grand Lodge of England."

Prince Hall, it appears, to some extent wanted to establish an independent Masonic government. At that time the general movement towards independent Masonic government for America "was fast gaining ground; and always the Negro Masons were ignored in any plans projected." (Prince Hall and His followers, Crawford, p.17). History also reveals that when the Grand Lodge of Washington agreed to give a partial recognition to Black Masons in that state, every Grand Lodge in this country and Canada cut their fraternal relation with the Washington Grand Lodge. The Grand Lodge of Massachusetts experienced a similar fate, when in 1947 its members voted to establish a limited cooperation and "mutual helpfulness" between white and Black Masons. This decision was withdrawn in 1949 because of threats to the Massachusetts Lodge from other Grand Lodges.

-155-

Masonic authorities consider Prince Hall Masons (Black Masonic Lodges) "clandestine Freemasons." This term refers to a body of Freemasons or of those improperly claiming to be Freemasons. In the 27th Chapter of the Masonic Quiz Book, the question is asked: "How do the Masonic authorities and Grand Lodges rate the status of Negro Lodges?" Answer: "They consider the assumption of authority by the Negro Grand Lodges as illegal Masonically, and therefore consider the entire organization clandestine." Whalen states that: "American Freemasonry is Jim Crow. Not only do Masons deny the legitimacy of Negro Masonic Lodges, but they refuse to initiate colored men into white lodges...Negroes may not enter or visit a white lodge or even converse on Masonic subjects with white men. (p.10). Albert Pike expressed his deep seated racism when he declared in 1868: "I took my obligation to white men, not Negroes. When I have to accept Negroes as brethren or leave Masonry, I shall leave it." Whalen also points out that "Girard College is usually claimed as a Masonic benevolence and it is instructive to note that Girard's will stipulated that no Negroes and no clergymen were ever to set foot on the campus." (p.12). It is further reported that most of the leaders of the Ku Klux Klan were Masons, and as already mentioned, J. Edgar Hoover was a Mason. His bitter hatred and vicious plots to destroy productive positive Black organizations is a matter of public record. In fact, I do not doubt that he recruited members from the Masonic organization to infiltrate the once Nation of Islam. It is also reported that he not only tried to destroy the civil rights movement, but he tried to drive Dr. Martin Luther King to commit suicide.

SECRECY AND SILENCE

The most important lesson in Masonry is secrecy and silence. From the time one enters the Masonic doors, the importance of secrecy is stressed. From the first degree to the last he bounds himself to a death oath of secrecy. In the first degree, he is pierced on his naked left breast with the point of the compass (this is called the Shock of Entrance). This is to teach him that "as this is an instrument of torture to your flesh, so should the recollection of it be to your conscience, should you ever presume to reveal any of the secrets of Freemasonry unlawfully." Many Masonic authorities argue that the existence of the Masonic institution is dependent on its secrecy. In fact, most of the Masonic signs allude to the penalty for revealing the Masonic secrets. For example, the Royal Arch Sign is made by drawing the right hand, (as in a salute) across the forehead. This, the ritual states, refers to the penalty of the degree--skull smote off. In the Royal Arch Oath, he says, "...binding myself under no less penalty than that of having my skull smote off and my brains exposed to the scorching rays of the noon day sun, should I violate this my solemn obligation as a Royal Arch Mason. So help me God." (Ronayne's Hand Book of Freemasonry, p.221).

Masonic secrecy supercedes all friendships and family relations. In the Masonic Book of Jurisprudence, all Masons are instructed not to discuss Masonry with their family, friends or strangers. It states, "You are to act as becomes a moral and wise man; particularly not to let your family, friends and neighbors know the concerns of the lodge...you shall be cautious in your words and carriage that the most penetrating stranger shall not be able to discover or find out what is not proper to be intimated, and sometimes you shall divert a discourse, and manage it prudently for the honor of the worshipful faternity." (Jurisprudence of Freemasonry, p.ccvi). On page 29 of the same book, it reads: "If divested of its secret character, it would lose its identity, and would cease to be Freemasonry...such change of its character would be social suicide and the death of the Order would follow its legalized exposure. Freemasonry, as a secret association, has lived unchanged for centuries. As an open society, it would not last for many years." Mackey states, "These virtues (secrecy and silence) constitute the very essence of all Masonic character; they are the safeguard of the institution, giving it all its security and perpetuity," (p.920).

In the fourth degree (Secret Master) the Mason is taught the sign of silence, which is made by placing the first two fingers of the right hand on the lips. It is answered by placing the first two fingers of the left hand on the lips. This sign alludes to the penalty of having "my tongue cut out at the roots, if I reveal the secrets of Masonry, unlawfully." In the thirty-third degree, the Mason is told that, "you may be ever ready to lay down your life for the triumph of the principles of our Rite." (Scottish Rite Masonry, Vol.2, p.471).

Why the secrecy? What is the big secret? What are you hiding? Some Masonic authorities claim that the only true secrets in Masonry are its passwords, signs, tokens and grips. Other non-Masonic and ex-Masonic authors have advanced the theory that the purpose of Masonic secrecy is rooted in its aim, for political, economic power and world dominance. Still others argue that Masonry is a Satanic organization and that if the covers were pulled off and the general public was exposed to its devilish practices, it would demand its total annihilation.

I believe that the secrecy is primarily based on the belief that the masses of people are basically ignorant, unfit and incapable of grasping the Wisdom of God and the science of creation. Therefore, only the "select and elect" are worthy of this knowledge. Those who have some knowledge of the Egyptian mystery systems know that only certain individuals were deemed "qualified" to receive admission into their secret schools. In the Masonic catechism of the first degree, the question is asked: "Why did your ancient brethren meet on high hills and low valleys?" Answer: "The better to guard against the approach of cowans and eavesdroppers ascending or descending."

Some Masons have attempted to reveal some of the secret works of Masonry by exposing the "passwords, grips, tokens and signs." Muhammad Amini and Sa'di Abu Habib explain, "Of its existence and of the continuance of its life has been broken by some Freemasons; some consciences were awakened by the dawn of truth which exposed what was intended for those ignorant stones" (p.19). Robertson argues, however, that "one can divulge only the dead letter, not the spirit, which of its own accord reveals itself to those who are privileged to understand." (Freemasonry and The Vatican, p.48).

CAPTAIN WILLIAM MORGAN

It is reported that in 1826 Captain Morgan became disillusioned with the Masonic Lodge and decided to write an "expose" on the Lodge. History tells us that this angered the Masons so much that they kidnapped him and took him to Fort Niagara. "He was never again seen alive but a body was later identified as his and the general public concluded that for once Masons had taken their obligation to protect their secrets and punish offenders in a serious rather than a symbolic sense." In rememberance of Captain Morgan, a thirty-eight foot monument was erected in Batavia, New York. Inscribed at the bottom of the monument are these words: "sacred to the memory of Wm. Morgan, a native of Virginia, a captain in The War of 1812, a respectable citizen of Batavia and a martyr of the freedom of writing, printing and speaking the truth. He was abducted from near this spot in the year 1826, by Freemasons, and murdered for revealing the secrets of their order."

If Morgan did in fact reveal the secrets of Masonry, why then has not it (Freemasonry) ceased to exist, as the Masonic Book of Jurisprudence states would happen? This tells us one or two things, (1) either Morgan never really revealed the true secrets of Freemasonry, because its true secrets are not at all revealed ever to the common Mason, or (2) Freemasonry can live without its cover of darkness

-159-

and secrecy. Perhaps it can bathe in the glorious light of openness and free expression.

"Know they not that Allah Knoweth what they conceal and what they reveal?" (Holy Qur'an, 2:77)

"He merges Night into Day and He merges Day into Night, and He has full knowledge of the secrets of (all) hearts." (Holy Qur'an, 57:6)

SYMBOLISM

Masons also refer to themselves as "builders." This title, Masonically, alludes to those workmen who participated in the construction of the Temple of Solomon. In Freemasonry the story of Solomon and the building of the Temple are so closely connected "that to attempt to separate the one from the other would be fatal to the further existence of Freemasonry." So imporant is the Temple of Solomon to Freemasonry that each Masonic Lodge is and must be a symbol of that Temple. Mackey's Revised Encyclopedia of Freemasonry states that "each Master in the chair representing the Jewish King; and every Freemason a personification of the Jewish Workman. Thus must it ever be while Freemasonry endures." (p.1022).

Although the most important event that took place during the building of the Temple (according to Masonry) was the tragic murder of Hiram Abiff, the Grand Master Builder, other aspects of this story are also of significant importance to Masons.

The Bible says there were two pillars at the entrance of the Temple, one on the right called Jachin, and one on the left called Boaz. (See I Kings 7:15-22, II Chronicles 3:15, 4:12-13.). According to Masonry these two pillars denote strength and establishment. "Taken together, they allude to a promise of God to David that He would establish His Kingdom in strength."

The building of Solomon's Temple, the materials used, the size, its measurements, etc. are all symbolic, and allegorically they allude to something more important, of greater significance. Mackey writes, "We must receive the myths and legends that connect it (Freemasonry) with the Temple, not indeed as historic facts, but as allegories; not as events that have really transpired, but as symbols; and we must accept these allegories and these symbols for what their inventors really meant that they should be--foundation of science of morality." (p.1023).

The Bible mentions a Temple that was built "without hands or the knocking of hampers". The Scripture also tells us that Solomon built the Temple for the glory of God (II Chronicles 6:2). He also acknowledged that God could not be contained in the Temple or the heavens of heavens (II Chronicles 6:18).

The wise Masons understand that the building of the Temple is symbolic of building the mind and spirit with truth and knowledge. During the initiation ceremony, the candidate is conducted up the "three, five, and seven steps" and between the two pillars of the Temple. What does the two pillars represent? In one sense they represent two personalities. The Bible says Boaz was a noble and just king. He was a compassionate man. In the Book of Ruth we read how he displayed his compassion and fair-mindedness in relations to Ruth the maid, who became his wife. (Ruth 2,3). Jachin, on the other hand, the Bible tells us only that he was the fourth son of Simeon. Other sources, however, say that the word Jachin is derived from two Hebrew words, "Jah", meaning "God", and "iachin", meaning "will establish". Some Masonic scholars point out that the Temple of Solomon represents the whole human body and that Boaz the left pillar symbolizes the sympathetic column and Jachin the spinal column that leads up to the brain. These pillars are also said to represent personal choice (Boaz) and Universal Law (Jachin). Steinmetz points out that the only reason for entering the Temple was to be in the presence of God, therefore, that person made a personal choice to come and submit to the Universal Law of God. He also says that the act of erecting the Temple is the development of character, the evolving of the real individual. Albert Pike explains the Temple and the two pillars as follows: "We no longer expect to rebuild the Temple at Jerusalem. To us it has become but a symbol. To us the whole world is God's Temple, as is every upright beast...Jachin and Boaz, that stand at the portals of the Temple built by wisdom, on one of which Masonry sets the celestial globe, symbol of the spiritual part of our composite nature, and on the other the terrestrial globe, symbol of the material pasta." (p.860).

In Masonry there is a symbol of a circle with a point in the middle and two parallel lines on its sides, one on the right and one on the left. Above the circle is a flying scroll. There are various meanings to this symbol. One of the meanings is in connection with the Temple of Solomon. The Circle represents the Universal law of God or the circumference of the Temple (which is the whole world), the point represents man, the two parallel lines allude to the two pillars Boaz and Jachin or the dual nature of creation, positive and negative, material and spiritual. Lastly the scroll represents the Word or Guidance of God. If we reflect a little further, we will notice that the human being has a temple which extends to both sides of the head. In Masonry, one of their signs is given by placing the fingers to the side of the head or the temple (Scottish Rite Masonry, Vol.II). The human being has two ears, one on the left and one on the right. Information is received through our ears, consciously and subconsciously. In connection with the two pillars, Boaz and Jachin, it can also be concluded that they represent conscious and the subconscious. **The Holy Qur'an says that Allah (God) has placed an angel on our right side and an angel on the left side to record all our actions. (H.Q.50:17-18). In Masonry these two angels are represented by John the Baptist and John the Evangelist. At the end of prayer (salat) the Muslim, after reciting both parts of the Tashahhud, turns his head to the right and says: As-Salaam Alaikum-wa-rahmatul-l-lah (peace be unto you and the mercy of God). Then he turns to the left and says the same greeting. This gives us balance and peace on each side. This brings us again to the double headed eagle of Freemasonry. One head faces the right and the other faces the left.**

Boaz and Jachin are also the names of two Masonic tokens or handshakes. In the first degree the candidate is taught to shake his brother's right hand by placing the thumb on the first knuckle which is called Boaz. As a Fellow Craft he places the thumb on the second knuckle (Jachin). This tells us that Boaz and Jachin also have something to do with the hands. The Masonic Encyclopedia says that the hand as a symbol holds a high place in Freemasonry because "it is the principal seat of the sense of feeling so necessary to and highly revered by Freemasons." The hands are a symbol of action or activity. The hands do the bidding or work of the mind. Jesus said, "**as you can tell a tree by the fruit it bears, so can you tell a man by his works**". The Qur'an says at the Judgment Day, man's "**hands will speak out against him**". We have two hands. Masonically the left hand represents the weaker side of man and the right hand represents the strong side of man. This tells us too then that Boaz, the left pillar of the Temple, was/is weaker than Jachin, the right pillar.

In the third degree the Master Mason is instructed to place his right hand (the stronger hand) over the left hand while taking his oath. In fact the Master Mason stands with his heels together and his right hand over his left against his stomach. The Muslim, when performing prayer, stands with the right hand over the left. This position is called Qiyam. Imam W. Deen Muhammad in explaining the meaning of Wudu (ablution) pointed out that, "the right hands are used to symbolize action, and the hand is symbolic of our conscious acts.... The left hand is symbolic of our impulsive or unconscious acts. These acts are subject to negative influences when our conscious acts are not rightly oriented." (Prayer and Al-Islam, p.72).

The Temple of Solomon, according to Masonic teachings, represents much more than a physical building located in Jerusalem. One Masonic writer says Solomon himself symbolizes the psychial or mental plane of man. He argues that this is evident by virtue of the fact that Solomon asked God for wisdom.

What else do we find at the building of Solomon's temple? We find in Freemasonry a story of the "Key Stone" that the builders rejected. It is based on the words of the Bible, "**The stone which the builders refused is becoming the head stone of the corner.**" (Psalms 118:22). According to the Masonic account of this story, it was the custom of King Solomon, during the building of the Temple, to have the workmen carry their work up for inspection. The work was inspected by three overseers stationed in the South, West and East. The legend says that on the sixth day of a certain week three craftmen went to present their work for inspection. Upon presenting their work the following dialogue took place: Junior Overseer said, "Who comes here?" Answer: "Craftsmen from the quarries with work for inspection." The first craftsman presented a square stone. According to the story, the overseer took the stone and applied his trying square to its corners and sides, then said, "This is good work, true work, square work, pass to the senior overseer." The second craftsman or workman then presented his work in the same manner as the first one. The overseer said the same thing to him also. When the third craftsman presented the keystone, the overseer applied his trying square, and finding that it did not fit its (the keystone) sides and angles exclaimed: "This is neither oblong nor square; neither has it the mark of any of the craft upon it, but owing to its singular form and beauty, I am unwilling to reject it, and will suffer it to pass to the senior overseer for further inspection." The story says that the three men then went to the west gate and presented their work in the same manner and received the same response. Lastly, they took their work to the master overseer, in the East. The ritual says, "On presenting it (the keystone) to the master overseer at the East gate, called together his brother overseers for consultation, remarking that it was neither oblong nor square, neither had it the mark of any of the craft, and they not knowing the mark that was upon it, concluded it unfit for use and agreed to heave it over among the rubbish." (p.62). On the Masonic Keystone is inscribed the initials H.T.W.S.S.T.K.S. (Hiram, The Widow's Son, Sent To King Solomon). Masonic legend says that this stone was prepared by Hiram Abiff before he was murdered.

The story says that the keystone was thrown into the rubbish of the temple. Hiram was first buried in the rubbish also. The message here, then, is that the keystone is connected or symbolizes Hiram or a particular aspect of the human being. Some Masonic authorities says that Hiram represents the generative power in man. Others say he represents a principle in the intellect. Hiram was one of the three chief figures in the building of the temple. Therefore, if the temple is symbolic of something else, then it should also follow that the three main characters, Solomon, Hiram King of Tyre, and Hiram Abiff, are also symbolic. Steinmetz says they represent material, mental and spiritual. Percival says they are symbolic of the Doer, Knower and Thinker in man.

A keystone is a stone that unites the two pillars as sides of an arch. It is really a uniting stone. Masonically, this stone united the two pillars, Boaz and Jachin. It unites the spiritual and the material. Prophet Muhammad, the model human being, is a good example of the keystone because through him the social life and the spiritual life were united. He established a balanced community. Imam W. Deen Muhammad in his latest book writes, "And what does the Qur'an say that was revealed to Prophet Muhammad (PBUH)? Allah said to the heavens (spiritual) and the earth (physical), 'Be you joined together willingly or unwillingly'... He said to the heavens and the earth, "Come you together, be reconciled again." Praise be to Allah.

So we know that the Qur'an came for the purpose, to reconcile the spiritual concepts with the material concepts. to bring back again the unity of the sciences where the spiritual concepts are not at odds with the material needs and material life." (p.66).

The keystone that was rejected can also be said to represent the flesh or physical nature of man. In Christian dogma, flesh is sinful. According to Christianity, man is born in sin. Flesh is rejected for spirit. After the death of Jesus, the Christian was made into an ascetic community. The followers of Jesus were given asceticism under the name of Catholicism. (Asceticism is the belief in the spiritual world, separating oneself from the worldly life).

On the other hand, we find the materialist who rejects the idea or belief in a spiritual reality. They say, "the only thing that exists is this material life. If we can't perceive it through one of the five senses, it does not exist." J. Munsell

Chase, in his book <u>The Riddle of The Sphinx,</u> writes concerning the rejected stone, "The spiritual nature is this stone. The man of inferior understanding and base nature rejects it as interfering with his pleasures."

In actuality, the keystone represents that principle which unites the spiritual and the material. Remember, the Bible says this rejected stone eventually became the headstone. In Freemasonry, this stone is not retrieved or found until the Temple is near completion. The Keystone is found by the Royal Arch Mason. Only those Masons who have advanced to the Royal Arch degree receive the knowledge of the Keystone. The Royal Arch degree is in many respects the most important degree in Masonry because the "Lost Word," which is the <u>Sacred Word</u> kept secret, is also found in this degree. The word "sword" is a play on the substitute word, the Secret word "mah-hah-bone", or the Sacred word. According to Masonry the word was lost during the building of the Temple and a substitute word was adopted.

Let us look at the wisdom of the Royal Arch degree. This degree consists of at least <u>nine</u> members. In the Royal Arch Examination, it reads: "Are you a Royal Arch Mason?" Answer" "I am that I am." Question: "How shall I know you to be a Royal Arch Mason?" Answer: "By three times three under a living arch and over a triangle..." Question: "How many compose a chapter of Royal Arch Masons?" Answer: "Nine or more." Question: "When composed of only nine, who are they?" Answer: "(1) The excellent High Priest, (2) Companions King, (3) The Scribe, (4) The Captain of the Host, (5) Principal Sojourner, (6) Royal Arch Captain, and the three Masters of The Veils." Question: "Whom do the first three represent?" Answer: "Joshua, Zerubbabel and Haggai."

Nine is the essential and most important number in this degree. The teachings of Freemasonry says that the Word could only be found by travelling through <u>nine</u> arches. In this degree the Thrice Puissant says to the candidate: "My brethren, when of old, the chosen three had traveled the nine arches, they came to a dome and beheld upon the cube stone the resplendant delta, on which the true name of the Great Architect of the Universe was impressed in letters of dazzling light. They fell on their knees, made the signs of admiration (by raising the hands to the sky, with the head leaning on the left shoulder) and exclaimed, 'Jehovah, as you have done.' But they were not able to pronounce the ineffable name." (p.264). According to the wisdom of this degree, nine ancient Grand Masters, eminent for their virtue, were chosen Knights of the Royal Arch, and shortly after were admitted to the Sublime Degree of Perfection." Let us look further at the number nine. The Masonic Encyclopedia states that in Freemasonry, "nine derives its value from its being the product of three multiplied into itself, and as a result in Masonic language, the number nine is always denoted by the expression three times three". For a similar reason, 27 which is 3 times 9, and 81, which is 9 times 9, are esteemed as sacred numbers in the advanced degrees. (p.709).

Imam Warith Deen Muhammad explained in his latest book, the symbolic meaning of the number nine. He says the number nine represents the union of the spiritual and the material, and that those with the knowledge of the nine actually have insight into the spiritual and the material realities of life. On page 53 of his book it reads, "So we have four as a square representing the material world, then we have five as a circle representing the spiritual world. Square = material conscience; Circle = spiritual conscience. If you take them both and put them together, they are symbolically placed under the number nine (4+5=9). Nine represents insight into the material reality and the spiritual reality. Now, can you see the significance of nine judges on the Supreme Court bench? If he has insight into the spiritual realities, he could handle any case; he should be able to handle any case. But if he is a wicked person, look how destructive, how dangerious he is. If he has that kind of knowledge and he is wicked, he is dangerous, very dangerous."

"That kind of consciousness is not accepted. Allah does not want us with that kind of consciousness. It is on the <u>Ninth</u> day of the Hajj that we meet with all the people. We meet all the brothers from all over the world, which means that if we expect to make progress in the ninth, if we expect to make material and spiritual progress, we are going to have to do it openly, not secretly." (IMAM W. DEEN MUHAMMAD SPEAKS FROM HARLEM) pg. 52-53

Where else do we find the <u>nine</u>? We find the nine in the circle of wisdom. A circle consists of 360 degrees, which is 3+6=9. We also find the nine at the top of the Scottish Rite Order of Freemasonry. This order consists of 33 degrees, which alludes to 3x3 which equals 9. What is Freemasonry saying? Freemasonry is saying that once a man completes his travel up the Masonic Pyramid, he received material and spiritual insight.

According to the old teaching of the Nation of Islam, the mystic man who called himself Master Fard Muhammad said that he traveled <u>nine</u> thousand miles. It was also said that he left after <u>three and a half years.</u> What is three and a half years? Three years and six months (3+6=9). Fard must have had the knowledge of the <u>nine.</u> **He did not use that knowledge for just ends. He used it to make African-Americans worship him and get the wrong idea of Islam. He said Islam is mathematics and mathematics is Islam. By applying certain mathematical techniques to his teachings, we arrive at the number nine.** What did he say about the wisdom of the Caucasians and the Black man? He said the Caucasian was evil and they only had thirty-three degrees of knowledge. Thirty-three is 3x3 which equals nine. On the other hand, he said the Black man was righteous and that he had 360 degrees of knowledge. 3+6=9. What was he saying? I understand this to mean that he was saying that the Caucasian has the same knowledge as the Black man, but he uses it for evil purposes. Let us return to the Royal Arch and the <u>Sacred Word.</u>

-169-

In the Royal Arch degree it says that man had to travel through the nine arches to get the Sacred Word. According to Freemasonry, this word is called the Tetragrammaton. Freemasonry says that this word could not be pronounced except by certain people at certain times. The Masonic Encyclopedia says, "Jehovah is, of all the significant words of Freemasonry, by far the most important. In Hebrew it consists of four letters (Yod -He-Vau-He) and hence is called the Tetragrammaton, or four letter name; and because it was forbidden to a Jew, as it is to a Freemason, to pronounce it, it is also called the Ineffable or Unpronounceable name." (p.501).

The tetragrammaton is derived from the word Tetractys, which means four. The word itelf is aplay on the number four. Professor Hilton Hotema in his book Tetragrammaton writes, "...Moreover, the Secret Word was never pronounced; it was spelled, and expressed in four words, which are the sacred words Yod-He-Vau-He." This four part word is also connected or corresponds to the four rivers that left the garden of Eden and became heads (Genesis 2:10), as well as the four beasts of the Bible (Revelation 4:6-7) and the four angels of (Revelation 9:14). This word more than anything alludes to the four basic elements of the universe: Earth, Water, Fire and Air. These elements dominate the physical or material world (matter). Four represents a square. the square represents the material realities. As we pointed out in a previous section, the square in most cases represents the material. Steinmetz also points out that four, the square, is a symbol of material things (p.120); so does Imam Warith Deen Muhammad (p.53); Albert Pike (p209, 861 and 58) and many others. We also find four at the base of the pyramid and in the figure of the Sphinx. Again, the four represents the four basic elements of the universe. Hotema writes, "The symbolical tetrad, represented in the Ancient Mysteries by the four forms of the Sphinx--man, eagle, lion and bull--corresponded with the four principle elements of the universe: earth, water, air and fire." He also adds, "Masons are still searching for that 'lost word', if they found it, they would not know it, for they do not know what they are searching." (The Mysterious Sphinx, p.10,11).

The Masons and Shriners are taught the significance of the four elements and its relationship to the Tetragrammaton (sacred word). In fact they have certain body signs that alludes to these elements. In the 29th degree (called the Knights of St. Andres or Patriarch of the Crusader), these elements are illustrated first by wiping your forehead with the back of the right hand, the head inclined forward (sign of earth). The second sign (water) is made by placing the right hand on the heart, then extending it outwards to about the height of the breast, let it fall on the right side of your body. The third sign (fire) is made by joining the fingers of both hands and then cover the eyes with the palms turned outwards. The last element (air) is illustrated by extending forward the right arm and hand at the height of the shoulder (See Scottish Rite Masonry, Vol. 2). These elements, according to Masonry and the science of symbolism, represent four essential aspects of man. In the 30th degree (called Grand Elect or Knight Kadash) it is stated that, "An intelligent man studies the secrets of nature. (Scottish Rite Masonry and Accepted Scottish Rite, Vol.2, p.280).

What then is the connection between the four part "word", the four elements and the human being? Professor Hotema in his book Tetragrammaton writes, "In the word which represented the four elements, we have found only part of the hidden meaning of the Mystic Symbolic Tetragrammaton. That part which we have found in the external aspect which deals with the four elements....A greater mystery is connected with the internal phase of the symbol, which dealt with the astral aspects that rise as the products of the functions of these four elements in the created body of man. These products are another one of the great mysteries of the universe. They appear as the astral qualities of (1) vitality, (2) consciousness, (3) mind, and (4) intelligence...." (p.26). In Masonry the internal meaning of the four elements are represented by the Pyramid. According to the ritual, the Pyramid is "that form of matter from which all other figures may be derived and which is an emblem of productive truth, varied order, and economic utility. It represents the true Mason who raised himself by degrees till he reaches heaven, to adore the sacred and unutterable name of the Great Architect of the universe."

Imam Warith Deen Muhammad pointed out during the early years of his leadership the symbolic meaning of these four elements. He said that earth was symbolic of the physical or material; water represents the moral nature of man; fire represents wisdom; and air is symbolic of the spiritual nature in man. He explained in a lecture as follows,

"When you look at this pyramid, you see a three sided figure. You see a triangle...But at the base it is a square. Now, why is this symbol so important in religion? And believe me it is, it would not be on your dollar if it wasn't important. **I think it is the Shriners who also have the pyramid....I have not belonged to any of the orders so they can not charge me with breaking an oath. I never gave an oath...**Now, at the base of this pyramid we see it has four corners. That is a square, and from the square rises up the angles forming the pyramid. The angles represent human development...the base represents creation, the fundamental principles in the development or in the creation. What are they? The elements of man: solid, water, air and fire. And out of these four elements the man develops."

"So they built the pyramid because they had this knowledge and they built the pyramid showing as a base these four elements. And in Egyptology these elements are called the 'four sons of Horus'...Look at the pyramid and you see an eye. Look on your dollar bill, you can see the eye there. What does that mean? It means that man is looking for vision. There is in human nature, the desire for vision." So the wise people know that vision is what we want. We want to see, so we begin from the base of the pyramid and we go up towards vision." (Jain, Jacobs and Metaphysics lecture, 1976).

According to Freemasonry, the Sacred Word is supposed to be the name of God. If that name Yod-He-Vou-He does in fact represent the four elements or four stages of human

-172-

development, then it can be concluded again that the God of Masonry is really the god of the physical world and not the creator of the heavens and the earth. On the other hand, if this four part word alludes to the knowledge or science of human nature, then it can be easily seen what the pyramid is a symbol of.

The mystic man Fard taught that God manifested in the physical creation. He also said, "Whoever could bring in four devil heads at one time, would receive a trip to the holy City Mecca to see brother Mahmoud." We can understand better now, in light of what Imam. W. Deen Muhammad has said about Fard, what was meant by that lesson. Fard chose Eli-Jah which means "a call to Jah." The word Jah according to Freemasonry is only an abbreviation of the word Jehovah or the Tetragrammaton. Fard was also calling African Americans to the same god of Masonry. The tetragrammaton also represents (1) human motivation, (2) human drives, (3) human sentiments, and (4) human aspirations. Imam Muhammad said, "Elijah is a means for reaching God. Eli-Jah, a means for reaching God. Which god? "Jah." So who was Fard Muhammad trying to bring this community, called the Nation of Islam, to? Was he trying to bring this community to Almighty God who created the heavens and the earth? No! He was trying to bring the community to Jah. And who is Jah? Natural motivation, natural human drives, natural human sentiments, natural human aspirations. You are not there yet. The nature is just being stimulated. He came to awaken the nature. He picked up the principles of the false people, the devil himself." (Shackles of Slavery, 1978).

In his latest book, <u>Imam W. Deen Muhammad Speaks From Harlem, New York,</u> he explains, "So we do not call the man in Al-Islam 'four'. We say that Allah has given man his needs in <u>four periods.</u> But the man is 'five'. The man is spiritual conscience." (p.56).

What else do we learn from the Royal Arch degree of Masonry? We learn that there were four vails at the outer courts of the Tabernacle of the Temple. The question is asked, "To what do they allude?" Answer: To the four principle tribes of Israel which bore their banners in the wilderness, Judah, Ephraim, Reuben and Dan, whose emblem were the Lion, the Ox, the Man, and the Eagle." It is also in this degree that the Mason learns much about Prophet Moses. He is actually made to imitate Moses. Symbolically, the Mason finds the "Ark of Covenant." Upon discovering the Ark, the High Priest opens it and finds four items therein: (1) Scrolls which are supposed to represent the "book of the law", (2) a pot of manna, (3) Aaron's Rod, and (4) a piece of parchment with a symbolic code written on it. This code is said to be the key to understanding the mysterious writing that appears on the top and side of the ark.

The Royal Arch degree highlights the four and the nine which equals thirteen (4+9=13). furthermore, this is the thirteenth degree of the Scottish Rite. What does thirteen represent? Before we discuss the significance of this number, let us look at some of the language of the fourth degree and the nineth degree of Freemasonry to see if there is anything in those degrees that corresponds with the things we have already discussed.

Fourth Degree: The fourth degree is called the Secret Master's Degree. According to Masonic teachings this degree originated with King Solomon, shortly after the completion of the Temple. The ritual says that Solomon chose seven of the most worthy and expert workers from the Craft and appointed them guards of the Sanctum Santorum, and the sacred furniture of the Holy Place. In this degree the lodge is decorated with black curtains and strewed with white tears. The leader of the lodge represents Solomon and is called "Most Powerful." The Warden is called Adoniram. Masonically speaking, it was Adoniram who was responsible for inspecting the workman ship at Mount Lebanon and he was the first Secret Master. The symbolic age for a Mason in this degree is 3x27=81 which equals 8+1=9. In the Opening Ceremonies, the Master of the lodge says: "Brother Adoniram, are you a Secret Master?" Adoniram answers: "Most Powerful, I have passed from the Square (materialism) to the Compass (spiritualism). I have seen the tomb of our respectable Master Hiram Abiff and have in company with my brethren shed tears thereat." Master of the lodge says: "What is the clock my brother?" Adoniram answers: "The dawn of day has driven away darkness, and the light begins to shine in the lodge".

In this degree, the candidate is prepared for initiation by having an apron tied over his eyes and a square placed on his forehead. He is led to the door of the lodge and instructed to give seven knocks. Adoniram asks: "Who knocks at the door of our Sanctuary?" The Master of Ceremonies answers for the candidate: "One who knows where the Acacia grows and would help us gather its fruit." The candidate is admitted and led to the Master of the Lodge (Solomon) who says: Brother Adoniram, I see this Master who seeks the sanctuary bears the square (materialsim) upon his forehead, and thereby gives assurance that reason rules his mind; but he is yet blind though he has learned to labor; shall he behold the resplendant name of God? " Adoniram says: "If he is willing to pronounce the oath which binds us all, we consent that he should be permitted to see the mystic name. The Master of the lodge says, "That name can be learned only by him who 'knows himself.'"

The Grand Orator says to the candidate: "The initials of the names you saw in the nine beams of the Shekinah are those which God gave himself when He spoke to Moses on Mount Sinai. He explains them as follows: Adonai (signifying Supreme Lord), Jehovah, Elohim (Supreme Judge), Als (Powerful), Shadai (Omnipotent), Yzebath (Lord of Hosts) Ozi (Mightiness), Gibour (Strength), Ahad (Only One).

On page 57 of the Scottish Rite Ritual we learn that the seven branched candlestick alludes to the seven planets. The Eye over the door of the lodge represents the Eye of God. There was only one door in the Holy of Holies of Solomon's Temple. The doors were called Zi Za and were located on the east side. The doors were covered with gold, purple, hyacinthe and azure, "which represented the four elements."

Now let us look briefly at the <u>ninth</u> degree. The ninth degree is called the Master Elect of Nine. According to the Masonic Bible this degree details the mode in which the murderers of Hiram Abiff received their punishment. The symbolic colors are red, white and black. On the flap of the apron is a picture of one bloody arm holding a dagger; and another bloody arm holding a bloody head is by the ear. In the ante-room there is a lamp, below the lamp in large letters is written the word "REVENGE." The meetings are called chapters. Members in this degree sit with their right leg over the left, the right elbow on the right knee, with the head resting in the palm of the right hand. The Master of the lodge (in all cases) represents Solomon, and the Warden is called Stolkin.

In the Opening Ceremonies, Solomon says to Stolkin: "Brother Inspector, what is the hour?" Stolkin answers; "Most Sovereign, the dog star rises in the east, followed by the Archer, and they are in pursuit of the serpent of Ignorance." Question: "Are you an Elected Knight?" Answer: "A lamp lighted me, a cave received me, and a spring refreshed me." During the initiation ceremonies, the candidate is instructed to give eight and one knocks on the lodge door. The question is asked: "Who knocks at the door of our Chapter to interrupt our deliberations?" Answer: "A stranger who demands to speak to the King privately." According to the ritual, Solomon consults with this stranger and then says to the brethren, "I have at this moment learned from this stranger that he has discovered an idividual concealed in a cave near the coast of Joppa, answering the description of one of the murderers of our lamented Master Hiram Abiff. He has also offered to conduct those I may select to the place of the concealment." The legend has it that Solomon chose nine men to go and search out the murderers. It says he appointed Joabert to lead the other eight. In the ritual, it reads "Faithful Joabert, I shall now select you as the ninth and last of the numbers. Pursue the murderer of our regretted Master Hiram Abiff, seek him, seize him and bring him here to suffer the penalty of his horrid crime." The candidate is made to initiate Joabert.

He (the candidate) is blindfolded and then conducted into a dark room with a little lamp. He is istructed to put his left hand on the table in the room and to lay his forehead on the back of the left hand, placing the right hand on his thigh. There is that partially lit room (which is supposed to represent a cave) he is instructed to, on the first knock, take off the blindfold. On the second knock, drink from a cup that is placed by his left hand. On the third knock he is instructed to take a knife and strike the villian first on the head and then on the heart. Cut off his head and take it in your left hand, the poniard in your right, and follow me."

The candidate is then asked a series of questions, some of which are: "What have you seen in the Cave?" Answer: "A light, a poniard and a fountain, with the traitor Akirap or Jubellum." Question: "Of what use were these to you?" Answer: "The light to dispel the darkness of the place, the dagger to revenge the death of our respectable Master Hiram Abiff, and the spring to quench my thirst." Question: "Where were you made a Master Elect?" Answer: "In the hall of audience in Solomon's palace." Question: "How many Masters Elected were made at that time?" Answer: "Nine of whom I was one." Question: "What motive prompted you to become a Master Elected?" Answer: "The desire of revenging the death of Hiram Abiff, by destroying his murderers." Question: "Where did you find the assassin?" Answer: "In the bottom of a cave, situated at the foot of a burning bush near Joppa, not far from sea." Question: "Who showed you the way there?" Answer: "An unknown person." Question: "What did the dark room represent?" Answer: "It is the representation of the cave where I found the traitor." Question: "How came you to be left there blindfolded?" Answer: "To call to my mind the traitor's sleep, and how often we may think ourselves secure after committing a crime, when we are in the most danger." Question: "What does the dog represent that you see in the Chapter on the road near the cave?" Answer: "The unknown person or the good citizen who conducted the Elected."

In closing the lodge on this degree, the Master of the lodge questions the warden as follows: Question: "What more is to be done? Answer: "Nothing, as everything is achieved, and Hiram Abiff avenged. Question: "Give me the pass word." Answer: "Begoal-Kal." Question: "What is the great word?" Answer: "Nekam." Question: "Is there no other pass word?" Answer: "Yes, there are two more by which we know one another, Joabert and Stolkin." Question: "At what time did the Elected set out for the cave?" Answer: "Just at dark." Question: "When did they return? Answer: "At day break." Question: "How old are you?" Answer: "Eight and one, perfect." Master says: "Brother, ignorance yields to our repeated vows. Let us advance in our labors".

In the fourth and ninth degrees we find, among other things, an important correlation with the 13th (Royal Arch), particularly as it relates to the significance of the numbers nine and four.

SYMBOLISM OF NUMBERS

The Number 13: The number thirteen is very important in Freemasonry and American symbolism. What does the number thirteen represent? It represents the 13 original colonies, which are alluded to on the back of the American dollar bill. On the American dollar bill we notice that there are 13 stars in the constellation above the eagle's head; 13 stripes on the escutcheon; 13 arrows in the eagle's talon; 13 leaves and 13 berries on the olive branch; and 13 letters in the motto "E Pluribus Unum." We also observe that there are 13 layers of stone in the pyramid, and 13 letters in the motto: "Annuit coeptis" which appears above the pyramid. The American flag also has 13 stripes on it.

Religiously or scripturally speaking, the number 13 represents Jesus and his twelve disciples; more specifically the gathering of those thirteen at the Last Supper (St. Mark 14:18). Symbolically, it means that Jesus was over, or mastered, the knowledge of the twelve, which actually represented the "spiritual" or heavenly plane. According to Masonic teachings, the twelve disciples are symbolic of the twelve zodiac signs which make up the heavenly disk. Pike gives the association on page 628 of his book Morale and Dogma. He writes, "What do you mean by the number 12? Answer: The twelve articles of Faith; the twelve Apostles, foundation of the Holy City, who preached throughout the whole world, for our happiness and spiritual joy.... The twelve signs of the zodiac, foundation of the Primum Mobile, extending it throughout the Universe for our temporal felicity." In the language of symbolism, the words sky, heaven, and spiritual are used interchangeably and refer to that which is above the material. Imam W. Deen Muhammad, during one of his powerful lectures entitled "Righteousness", explained the connection between the twelve disciples and the twelve zodiac signs in these words: "Actually, the sign that they have in their religion (Christianity), or the rule in their religion is referring to the sky. ...I am talking about the Last Supper. The Last Supper was not an earthly supper, it was a "sky" supper. The symbolic reference in the twelve is a reference to the twelve zodiac signs. And the zodiac, as you know, is a description of the heavenly disk...and Jesus Christ was the 13th one... He was really over the twelve. His job was to lead the twelve into the Kingdom..."

Godfrey Higgins, in his book <u>Anacalypsis</u> asserts that "The number of the twelve apostles, which formed the retinue of Jesus during his mission, is that of the signs, and of the secondary genii, the tutelar gods of the zodiacal signs which the sun passes through in his annual revolution." (p.781). The Bible says Jesus was the "light of the world." Physically speaking, the sun is the light of the world. Therefore, symbolically, Jesus, like the sun, had to pass through the twelve zodiac signs represented by the disciples. The Holy Qur'an says concerning the zodiacal signs: "It is We who have set out the zodiacal signs in the heavens and made them fair seeming to (all) beholders." (6:16).

The thirteen in one sense represents one who has knowledge of the spiritual, the upper or heavenly twelve. We also read in scripture, however, of another twelve, which represents the material or earthly plane. The scripture says there were twelve tribes of Israel. The Bible says the Children of Israel built a god of material (the golden calf). And the Holy Quran says, "**Allah caused water to come forth from a rock for the twelve tribes of Israel**" (2:62). The Hermetic philosophy says "As above, so below", that which is above is also beneath. Therefore, if the twelve disciples represent the upper or spiritual, then the twelve tribes are symbolic of the material or lower twelve. We also observe that a foot equals twelve inches, and that the ruler which is used to draw straight lines from point to point consists of twelve inches.

The Bible also says that on Jesus' return he would have the knowledge of the spiritual and the material. He would have spiritual and material insight. In the book of Revelation, it says that the twenty-four elders all would submit to him and lay their crowns down at his feet. "**And the four and twenty elders fell down and worshipped him** that liveth forever and ever" (Revelation 5:14). The book of Revelation then gives us a picture of twenty four bowing to one which equals twenty-five (24+1=25). What did we learn in the symbolic teachings of Fard Muhammad? He said there were twenty-four scientists, twelve major and twelve minor, that one from among the twenty-four became the god or ruler. He also said that the twenty-four corresponded to the circumference of the earth.

On page 108 of the book <u>Message to The Blackman in America,</u> it reads "There is a significance to the number 24 scientists and the 25,000 years. The number twenty-four scientists used is in accordance with the hours in our day and the measurement of the circumference of our planet around the Equator and the region of our poles, Arctic and Antarctic Oceans. Our planet is not exactly 25,000 miles in circumference, it is 24,896 and we, according to astronomy, do not have a full 24 hour day, but that of 23 hours, 56 minutes, and 46 seconds. The change made in our planet's rotation at the Pole is about one minute a year and takes 25,000 years to bring about complete change in the region of the Poles." In the book <u>Our Savior Has Arrived,</u> the Honorable Elijah Muhammad said that Fard taught him that the wisdom of each god "has a cycle of <u>twenty-five</u> thousand years. Once every twenty-five thousand years, another god would be given a chance to show forth his wisdom to the people." (p.98).

Twenty-five represents completeness, wholeness, perfection. The number twenty-five is really like the number seven (2+5=7). As we discussed earlier, seven represents completion also. The Bible says Samuel was a complete man, he was seven. A complete week consists of seven days. We can also conclude that when Fard said that the gods' wisdom only lived for twenty-five thousand years, he was only saying it lived until it reached its completion or fullness.. The Bible says, "Until the fullness of the Gentile be." (Romans 2:14) Further evidence that twenty-five is symbolic of completion and perfection is found in the history and language of Freemasonry. According to the history of Masonry, before its rites expanded to thirty-three degrees, it only consisted of twenty-five degrees. It was then called the "Rite of Perfection" or the "Grand Lodge of Perfection". The Masonic Bible states, "In 1758, a body was organized at Paris called the 'Council of Emperors of East and West.' This council prepared a Rite called the 'Rite of Perfection' which consisted of twenty-five degrees, the highest being the 'Sublime Prince of Royal Secret.'"

Since we arrived at the number twenty-five, by way of the numbers 13, 12 and 25, perhaps it would be wise to also examine these degrees. We have already discussed the 13th degree (Royal Arch).

MASONIC DEGREES

12th Degree: This degree is called the Grand Master Architect. According to the Masonic authority Albert Pike, this degree is designed to "bring us at once to reflect upon the dignity of human nature, and the vast powers and capacities of the human soul." this degree is strictly a scientific degree. It focuses on the the principles of architecture and the connection of the liberal arts with Freemasonry. Meetings in this degree are called a chapter. The Lodge room is decorated with white and red curtains and "furnished with the five orders of architecture, and a case of mathematical instruments." The officers are King Solomon (referred to as Most Powerful) and two Wardens (called Grand Inspectors).

In this degree the candidate is made to represent Joabert, the favorite of Solomon. In the opening ceremonies the Master of the Lodge inquires: What is your duty Brother Inspector? Answer: "Most Powerful, the Chapter is well tyled and the profane cannot penetrate into our mysteries." Question: Are you a Grand Master Architect? Answer: "I know what is contained in a perfect case of mathematical instruments." Question: What is contained in a perfect case of mathematical instruments. Question: What is contained in a simple case? Answer: "A compass with five points, a parallel rule, a scale, or compass of proportion, a protractor, on which are engraved 180 degrees." Question: Where were you received an Architect? Answer: "In a white place figured with flames." Question: What do they mean? Answer: "The white signifies the purity of the heart, and the flames the zeal of the masters." Question: What do the stars in the North mean? Answer: "That virtue should guide every Mason in his actions, as the North Star does for the mariner in his navigation."

After the Lodge is opened and the candidate is prepared for initiation, the Master of Ceremonies gives three knocks on the lodge door for the candidate. Responding to the inquiry from within, the Master of Ceremonies replies (for the candidate): "Brother Joabert, not being satisfied with the knowledge he has already attained, and the dignities conferred on him, finds he cannot measure distance beyond the reach of his limbs, nor can he find his path through darkness, or in unknown places." The candidate is then conducted to the East where he is questioned about the previous degrees. The Most Powerful says: Are you a Secret Master? Candidate replies: "I have the honor of being received and acknowledged as such." Question: Are you a Perfect Master? Answer: "I have seen the circles and the square placed on the two columns across." Question: Are you an Intimate Secretary? Answer: "I am" (lifting up his eyes). Question: Are you a Provost and Judge? Answer: "I have distributed justice impartially to all the workmen." Question: Are you an Intendant of the Building? he five steps of exactitude, I have penetrated into the inner parts of the temple, I have seen the Hebrew character, the mysterious J's without knowing what they meant." Question: Are you an Elected Master of Nine? Answer: "The ballot alone has determined that matter and I have been made acquainted with the cave." Question: Are you an Illustrious Elected of Fifteen? Answer: "My zeal and my work have procured me this degree." Question: Are you a Sublime Elected Knight? Answer: "My name (Emeth) will inform you".

The candidate is then instructed to take his oath, after which he is given a pass word (Rab-banaim) and a sacred word (Adonai). The Master of the lodge then teaches him the use and meaning of several instruments. He says: "Upon the altar now before you, behold a case of mathematical instruments." They are the parallel ruler, the tracing dividers, the scale of parts, the sector, and the protractor. He explains the significance of each instrument as follows:

The Parallel Ruler enables us to draw two lines equal distant from each other at every point, so that they never can meet, which signifies that the agreement of the words of the Grand Architect is determined by means of equalizing opposition of forces; and hence, that in human government the division and balancing of powers is essential.

The Tracing Dividers enables us to draw distinct and perfect circles and to mark the points they give us. This signifies that we must have a distinct design before we act.

The Scale of Parts enables us to make all our designs proportionate, so that all the parts and incidents will agree together in fulfilling the object we seek to accomplish. This signifies that truth in self consistent and every distinct truth agrees with all other truth, hence so that one deed may not ultimately clash with another.

The Sector enables us to adapt our proportion to the limits assigned. This teaches us to reduce our designs to the measure of our means and time.

The Protractor enables us to draw angles from a given point and to protract and measure lines at all distances. This shows the necessity of having a fixed and sure beginning in order to discover truth, or to act with confidence.

After the Master of the Lodge finishes elaborating on the meaning of the instruments, the lodge is then closed.

24th Degree: The title of this degree is "Prince of the Tabernacle." It is intended to illustrate the order and direction given to Moses for building a Tabernacle at Sinai as described in the 25th Chapter of Exodus. (Richardson's Monitor of Freemasonry, p.180). "The ceremonies represent an invitation into the mysteries of the Mosaic tabernacle."

In this degree the lodge is called a Hierarchy and consists of two "apartments". The first one is termed a "vestibule" and is where the members cloth themselves. It is ornamented with various Masonic symbols and emblems. The second apartment is made circular by means of the hangings (curtains). In the middle is a chandelier with seven branches, each holding seven lights. The officers of the lodge are as follows: Most Potent and Powerful Prince, representing Moses the Lawgiver, stationed in the East. There are three wardens, the first represents Aaron, the High Priest, stationed in the West; the second warden represents Bezabeel and sits in the South; the third warden represents Ahaliab, the son of Ahisamach, stationed in the North. The candidate represents Eleazar son of Aaron.

In the opening ceremonies the duties of a Prince of the Tabernacle are explained by Aaron as such "To labor incessantly for the glory of God, the honor of his country and the happiness of his brethren." Each officer then explains his duty and the moral message which it alludes to. For example, the office who represents Ahaliab says: "I represent Ahaliab, who aided in the building of the first Tabernacle as a engraver, beautifying the vessels thereof, and as a embroiderer in blue and purple, and scarlet and fine linen. This teaches me to engrave upon my heart and ever recollect the laws of God and the statute of righteousness, virtue and truth, and to make my life beautiful with the embroidery of good actions."

Once the lodge is opened and the candidate is prepared for initiation both physically and by declaring that he seeks the hidden mysteries not "by any spirit of idle curiosity or the pride of knowledge but by a sincere desire to serve God and to labor for the reformation of mankind", the Senior Deacon is then instructed to explain the meaning of several symbols that are found in the lodge.

The Perfect Cube: is a symbol of the enlightened to whom they are known.

The Rough Stone: represents the profane, who

are ignorant of its mysteries.

The Three Lights: on the East, West and South of the altar represent the summer solstice, and the vernal and autumnal equinoxes.

The Two Columns: represent those erected by Enoch to perpetuate the history of the times before the flood.

The Level: is a symbol of equality and equanimity and teaches us that all men are equal in the sight of God and in the mysteries.

The Plumb: is a symbol of decision, firmness and independence; of truth and straightforward simplicity.

The Square: is a emblem of rectitude of intention and action, and obedience to constituted authority.

The Compass: is an emblem representing the command of the motion of the heavenly bodies, of harmony and of eternity.

The Triangle: with the (Hebrew) letter Yod in the center, suspended in the East, is an emblem of the Diety and of equity, because its sides are equal and it is the first perfect figure that can be formed with straight lines.

After the candidate receives a brief explanation of these symbols, he is led to the door of the second apartment. The senior Deacon gives seven knocks for the candidate on the door. The Junior Deacon opens the door and says: Who seeks admission to this inner chamber of the mysteries? Answer: Eleazar, the son of Aaron, who having been appointed to minister unto God in the Priest's office, desires first to know the mysteries and receive the indispensable degrees of Prince of the Tabernacle. The Junior Deacon then asks the Senior Deacon: By what further right does he (the candidate) expect to gain admission? Answer: By the sacred word Yod-He-Vau-He.

After the brief dialogue of the door of the second apartment, the candidate is admitted into the room "in due form." What is this "due form"? Due form in this degree means that the candidate is to be tested by the four elements mentioned earlier, fire, water, earth and air. Again, in this degree, the elements correspond with the so-called sacred word Yod-He-Va-He. On page 133 of the Scottish Rite Masonry Illustrated, it reads, "Then the Junior Deacon stops him (candidate), bares his right arm, holds a lighted candle near enough to it to cause him to feel the heat, and says, ' I test thee by fire.' The candidate is then conducted slowly three times around the room where he is stopped in the south and a small quantity of water is poured on his head. the warden representing Bezebel says: 'Thou hast reached the South, I test thee with water, the second test. Let it ever remind thee that none but the pure of heart can be admitted ot the Holy Tabernacle in the heavens.' Next the candidate is conducted to Aaron in the West, who instructs him to kneel on some sand and gravel. Aaron says: 'Thou has reached the West, I test thee with earth. It is the common mother, and to it our frail bodies return.' Lastly, the candidate is led to Moses in the East, who says: 'Thou has reached the East, I test thee with air, the life of all men; the free inestimable gift of God.'

When the tests are over, the Master of the lodge turns to the Senior Deacon and asks: Whence come you? Answer: "Out of darkness." Question: And whether go you? Answer: "To the East, the place of light and cradle of mysteries." Let us reflect briefly on this last statement. Without going into much detail, I would like to remind the reader that history tells us that although some Masons and others traveled east to Egypt and other ports of Africa, sincerely seeking knowledge, that Napoleon, Alexander the Great and other European conquerors traveled to the East not to seek knowledge, but to rob and destroy. According to History, Napoleon, a Master Mason, in a rage of jealously and bitterness, commanded his soldiers to destroy the African features of the Sphinx, so that its true image would be forever lost. George G.M. James in his book Stolen Legacy explains,

-187-

the Greeks went into Egypt and stole the wisdom of the Africans and claimed it to be theirs. He writes, "Egypt was the center of the body of ancient wisdom, and knowledge, religion, philosophical and scientific spread to other lands through student initiates. Such teachings remained for generations and centuries in the form of tradition, until the conquest of Egypt by Alexander the Great, and the movement of Aristotle and his school to compile Egyptian teaching and claim it as Greek Philosophy." (p.12-13)

Returning back to the 24th degree of Masonry after the Senior Deacon says he is going East, the place of light and cradle of mysteries, the Master of the Lodge says: "Thou art already there, what is thy desire?" Answer: "That this candidate may go the way that we have gone before him. The candidate is then conducted to the altar, where he takes an oath of secrecy. Next the candidate is taught how to give the Prince of the Tabernacle Sign of Recognition: This is made by placing the right hand open over the eyes, the left hand on the chest, then place the right hand to the left shoulder, and bring it down diagonally to the right side. (This is also called the sign of the scarf).

The candidate is also taught the Grand Sign, which is made as follows. Place both hands open upon the head, join the two thumbs and the two forefingers by their extremeties, forming a triangle. He is instructed to make six equal steps and one longer step.

After the candidate receives all his instructions, the Master of the lodge along with the other officers enters into a brief dialogue and then declares the lodge closed. (See Scotch Rite Masonry Illustrated, Vol.2 and Richardson's Monitor of Free Masonry).

25th Degree

This is an extremely important degree in Freemasonry. Masons of the degree are called "Knights of the Brazen Serpent." The traditions of this degree is founded upon the events described in the Book of Numbers in the Bible Chapter 21 verses 6-9. The Masonic Bible states, "The legendary origin of the degree is that it was established during the Crusades, in the land of Palestine, as a military secret society for the purpose of gratuitously caring for sick and wounded travelers, protecting them from the ravenges of the Saracens and escorting them to their destination." The meetings are styled, and the court of Sinai Richardson notes that this degree illustrates the Brazen Serpent set up by Moses in the wilderness. The officers are Most Powerful Grand Master, representing Moses seated in the East. The Senior Warden, representing Joshua, stationed in the north and the Junior Warden representing Aaron, sitting in the West. All the other members are called Knights. The candidate represents a Traveler."

During the opening ceremonies the Grand Master explains: Let the seven mystics light dispel the darkness of their count. The seven lights, masonically represent first the moon, second Mercury, third Venus, fourth Saturn, Fifth Jupiter, sixth, Mars and Seventh, the Sun. According to the opening ceremonies of this degree there are seven angels that preside over these seven lights. Namely (I) Saphael, the messenger of God; (2) Raphael, the healing influence of God (3) Hamaliel, the merciful kindness of God (4) Michael, the semblance and image of God (5) Gabriel, the strength and mightiness of God; (6) Auriel, the light and fire of God, and (7) Zerachiel, the rising of God, the sun of righteousness.

After the lodge is opened, the candidate is prepared for initiation, the stage is set, all the actors take their places. The candidate is blind folded and loaded with chains. He is then conducted to the door of the lodge and instructed to give five slow, three quick, and one knock. The Junior

Deacon asks: "Who comes here?" Answer: "One of the people of Israel, to announce to the Most Powerful Grand Master a great misfortune that has befallen the people and to implore at his hands relief and assistance." After further inquiry, the Senior Deacon explains that the candidate is from the tribe of Reuben, loaded with chains in token of the penitence of the people who flee in terror before the venomous serpents that Adonai hath sent to punish them. According to the Ritual, when this information is passed on to the Grand Master, he replies "Disobedient race; have they again tempted his anger?" The Grand Master turns towards the candidate and says: "Have you also murdered and called upon the false gods?" The candidate replies: "I have not, but because I refused and withstood the people, and rebuked them in the name of Adonai, they sought to slay me, but repenting they sent me hither because I had not sinned like them." Near the conclusion of the initiation ceremonies, the Grand Master gives the candidate a serpent of brass entwined round a Tau cross with his head elevated above it. He then says, "Take thou, therefore, Eleazar the High Priest, this serpent and cross and place it upon a pole and set it in the middle of the camp; and make proclamation that those who look upon it, confessing their sins and having faith in the Most High God, though they have been bitten by the venomous serpent, shall not die, but live, for Adonai is the God of mercy." He also says to the candidate while handing him the symbol: "I give it to you, my brother, that it may be evermore a symbol of faith, repentance and mercy, which are the great mysteries of man's destiny, and lest the knowledge of its true symbolic meaning should be lost." The candidate is then taught the signs, tokens and words of this degree.

Sign of Recognition: Cross the arms on the breast and incline the body forward as if to kneel on one knee.

Sign of Order: Incline the head downwards, and point to the ground with the forefinger of the right hand.

Token or Handshake: Place yourself on the right of the brother, and take his left wrist with your left hand.

Answer: He then takes your right wrist with his right hand.

Pass Word: I.N.R.I.

Covered Word: Johannes Ralp.

Sacred Word: Moses

In closing, the Grand Master inquires: "What is the hour?" Answer: "The twilight, after sunset." Grand Master: "Then it is time to close this court".

IMPORTANT CONCEPTS IN FREEMASONRY

In concluding this chapter, we will briefly discuss some important concepts and statements that are mentioned in the 8th, 28th, 30th, 32nd and the 33rd degrees of Freemasonry. We will also present some of the Masonic symbols and their meanings. Lastly, we will turn our direction to Makkah and analyze briefly some of the symbols that we find there.

In the Holy Qur'an, Allah says, **"Mautu fa hayaa"** (Die, that you may live). In the eighth degree of Masonry we find this same idea mentioned. During the initiation ceremonies, the candidate (called Joabert) is told by the Master of the Lodge "that in your present posture (lying position) you are made to take the place of the deceased master (Hiram Abiff); hence it is that we consider you as 'dead to sin and vice' and hope to see you 'alive to virtue and truth.' The Quranic verse tells us, and Imam Warith Deen Muhammad pointed out in his recent book, "death is a pre-condition or an antecedent state for life." (Imam W. Deen Muhammad Sepaks from Harlem, NY, p.92). He also pointed out that the right conception of life will cause us to die to our misconception of life. In order to come alive to truth and righteousness, we must die, or give up falsehood and corruption. According to the Bible, Jesus told Nicodemus the same thing. He said, **"you must be born again."** The Masonic legend of Hiram Abiff, concerning his death and resurrection is symbolic of this same idea "**Mautu fa hayaa**" (**Die, that you may live**). The Qur'an gives us straight and clear guidance; it goes directly to the point. The Mason does not come to this idea or meaning of Hiram's death until he reaches the eighth degree. Most of them do not advance beyond the third degree, therefore, most of them wouldn't receive the understanding that is concealed in the Hiramic legend. Albert Pike asserts that, "The symbols and ceremonies of Masonry have more than one meaning. They rather conceal than disclose the truth." (Morals and Dogma, p. 148).

If the symbols and ceremonies of Freemasonry are used to conceal rather than reveal the truth, as Mr. Pike states, then it is guilty of deception. The Holy Qur'an says, "**and cover not truth with falsehood, nor conceal the truth when you know (what it is)**". (HQ 2:42)

Prophet Muhammad (PBUH) said, "**It is better to teach knowledge one hour of the night than it is to pray all night.**" The Prophets were teachers, they were educators. The Bible says, Jesus used parables to bring the people to truth and understanding, he also said, "**These things have I spoken unto you in Proverbs; but the time cometh when I shall no more speak unto you in proverbs, but I shall shew you plainly of the Father.**" (John 16:25). In the twenty-eighth degree of Freemasonry (called Knights of the Sun) we read, "Mankind are so full of error and falsehood that though they search for happiness, few have knocked at the door of true light, which conducts us to felicity."

The Knights of the Sun are instructed to go among men and to use their best efforts to inspire them with a knowledge of truth, which is the pure source of all perfection." How can they inspire humanity with a knowledge of truth, if the masons have not the truth themselves. Pike says the candidate is deliberately misled. The symbols and ceremonies "conceal rather than reveal the truth." We also read further in the same degree that the Knight of the Sun must swear not to inspire humanity with the knowledge of truth that he receives. He says, "I promise and swear never to reveal any of the secrets of the degree of Knights of the Sun...should I willfully violate this my obligation, may my brethren seize me and thrust my tongue through with a red hot iron, to pluck out my eyes and deprive me of smelling and seeing, to cut off my hands and expose me in that condition in the field to be devoured by the voracious animals..." You cannot trust people who designed a system like this. In one instance they tell you to speak the truth, while in the same breath they threaten you with death if you speak the truth.

In the twenty-eighth degree the two officers are called Father Adam and Brother Truth. The Qur'an tells us that when the Creator told Adam to teach the angels, he did not conceal the message, he followed his instructions (HQ 2:33). According to the teaching of Prophet Muhammad, Father Adam was at the foundation of heaven, the first level. (Hadith Muslim and Bukhari). The Qur'an also says, Adam learned from his Lord words of inspiration, and his Lord showed him mercy. (HQ 2:37). The dialogue of the eighth degree, Father Adam says to Brother Truth, "whom do you conduct?" Answer: "A commander of the Temple, who desires to go out of darkness and to see the true light, and to know the true light in all its purity, and to ask tidings of the times that are promised to man." Question: "What more dost thou desire?" Answer: "To divest myself of original sin and renounce the juvenile prejudices of error which all men are liable to; namely the desire of all worldly attachments and pride.

According to the teachings of the Holy Our'an all of the angels submitted to Adam. In this degree (28th) that same message is given, except in a slightly different way. The seven angels that were mentioned in the twenty-fifth degree, reappear again in this degree. According to the Masonic Ritual, Father Adam orders the angels each to give the candidate a symbol or sign and explains its significance to him. They explain:

Three lights or candles: are indicative of Analysis, Synthesis, Analogy; the instruments of thought, and look for knowledge with a clear and fearless eye, and great truth wheresoever you meet her, whether on a throne or in a dungeon, triumphant or prescribed.

2. Caduceus: A symbol of peace "blessed are the peace-makers, for they are the children of God".

3. The Cone or Pyramid: is a emblem of productive truth, varied order and economic utility. It represents the true mason who raises himself by degrees till he reaches heaven, to adore the sacred and unutterable name of the Great Architect of the universe. If any will not work, neither should they eat.

4. The Goblet: Let the perfect purity of its content be a token of the resolution of this house, blessed are the pure in heart.

5. The World Globe: Let this globe be an emblem to remind you of true liberty, for though perfectly regular in form, though it measures equally in every direction it has no boundaries of lines of limitation; where the spirit of the Lord is, there is liberty.

6. The Cross: It is the sign of the sacred dogma of equality, and with it for a monitor we may yet hope for the reign of God on earth. "The meek shall inherit the earth".

7. The Ardent Dove Indicates that his soul will ever cherish affection for his fellow man.

Father Adam teaches the candidate the sign of a Knight of the Sun. The first sign is made by placing the right hand flat upon the heart, the thumb separate, so as to form a square. The answer sign is made by raising the right hand, and with the index finger pointing to the sky. "This is to show there is but one God, the source of all truth." (Richardson's Monitor of Free-Masonry, p. 186). It is interesting to note that the Muslim also raises his index finger signifying the oneness of Allah.

Many Muslims also place their right hand on their heart when they greet one another.

30th Degree

The thirtieth degree of Freemasonry is perhaps the most controversial degree, as far as Christians and non-Masons are concerned. This degree teaches the candidate to seek vengence for the execution of Jacques de Molai, whose order, the Knights Templars, was excommunicated by Pope Clement 5th, and who was himself along with fifty-nine of his followers burnt at the stake by order of the French King in 1314. In the opening ceremonies of this degree the Thrice Puissant Grand Master says to the First Lieutenant Grand Master: "What is your age?" Answer: "A century and more." Question: "Whom do you know?" Answer: "Two wretches." Question: "What is the object of our assembling?" Answer: "The hope of punishing crime." Addressing the candidate, the Master says:

"Reflect on the importance of your obligation and on the dreadful consequences which perjury might bring upon your head. Nothing could save you from the punishment which we would have full right to inflict. As already stated, we have no more to do with symbols of more or less significance, it is truth, it is reality we have now before us. Our statues are dreadful! We demand of you nothing contrary to the law of honor. But if you have discovered the object we have in view; if you have an idea of the end at which we aim, you will easily understand the importance of secrecy. You are now bound by your word of honor, and you may still retire. But one step more, and you are bound to us forever and at the peril of your life."

In most cases the candidate proceeds further. The ritual states, "In almost all the rituals of this degree, nothing but vengeance is spoken of."

During the initiation ceremonies, three skulls are placed on a table in the lodge. One of the skulls is crowned with a tiara, one wreathed with a laurel, and the third one a regal crown. The candidate is given a knife and is instructed to stab each skull. The Master of the Lodge takes each crown and throws them on the floor, he then steps on them and instructs the candidate to do the same. The regal crown he says, "My brother is the emblem of hypocrisy and tyranny. It represents the crown of Philip the Fair, King of France." The tiara, he explains, "represents the Tiara of the cruel and cowardly Pontiff, who sacrificed to his ambitions the illustrous order of those knights templars of whom we are the true successors. A crown of gold and precious stones ill befits the humble head of one who pretends to be successor, the Vicar of Jesus of Nazareth. It is therefore the crown of an imposter." It is no wonder that the Catholic church up until recently forbide its members to become Masons.

J. Blanchard in his Philosophical Analysis of the 30th degree writes, "This degree, and almost every other, professes to war and despotism. Yet Masonry is the completest despotism on earth; the edicts of a Grand Lodge must be obeyed without examination...Why this very ritual gives the Master power to stop and adjourn any debate, by three raps with the pomel of his sword! No slaves on a Southern plantation were ever bound by the laws of property to a more object, cringing obedience to their master than these Masons are to theirs." He further points out how this degree quotes Christ's law of equal love to our neighbor, and yet tells the candidate after he is received, "The slightest indiscretion will cost you your life"; that is, he says, they will kill him (candidate) if he lets out their secrets; tells the truth, by error, "indiscretion," or mistake. If this is not Masonic scoundrelism, what is scoundrelism! (Scottish Rite Masonry Illustrated, Vol.2, p.285).

Now, let us conclude by briefly discussing the last two degrees of Masonry, the thirty-second and the thirty-third.

The thirty-second degree is called the Sublime Prince of the Royal Secret. It is known as the military degree of Masonry and its meetings are called "Consistories". The Pass Words are: Phaal-Kal (which means separated0, Pharash Kas (reunited), Nikam Makah (calamity or revenge), Shaddai (the strong, the mighty).

The Sacred Words: Salix, Noni and Tengu. The motto of this degree is in Latin, "Spes mia in Dio est" (which means My hope is in God). Albert Pike in his instructions to the Mason of this degree, explains the meaning of the true Word of the Master Mason as follows: "Man in one, though of a double nature; and he attains the purpose of his being only when the two natures that are in him are in joint equilibrium; and life is a success only when it too is in harmony, and beautiful, like the great Harmonies of God and the Universe.

"Such, my Brother, is the true word of a Master Mason; such the true Royal Secret, which makes possible and shall at length make real, the Holy Empire of true Masonic Brotherhood." (Morals and Dogma, p. 861).

The 32nd degree inculcates all of the lessons of the previous degrees and gives a brief summary of those degrees. The degree is also important because it prepares the candidate for admissions into the "Mystic Shrine". The Commander in Chief says to the candidate, "Have you learned the first lesson? Have you fitted yourself to command, by first learning how to obey? Are you ready now, and always hereafter, to obey the lawful orders of this Grand Consistory and its Illustrious Commander in Chief?"

The Master of Ceremonies now tells the candidate that the 32nd degree of the Ancient and Accepted Rite of Freemasonry is the military organizaton. He then takes him to the various "camps" and explains to him the meaning of the symbols that are there. (It should be noted that each camp or tent is supposed to house the member of the various degrees. For example, in tent #9, the Apprentices, Fellow Crafts and Master Masons are housed). He also gives a brief explanation on all the degrees from the first to the thirty-first as follows:

First Degree: Shows you man, such as nature has made him, with no other resources than his physical strength. The inmost meaning of the first degree is man subjugated and struggling toward freedom, blinded by superstition, destitute of knowledge, defenseless and with the chains of despotism round him. He knocks timidly at the door of Masonry, is received, sworn to secrecy and made to stand upright in the middle of the lodge, as a man; as a man! Before then he was half naked, and half clad, neither barefoot nor shoed, half freeman and half slave.

Second Degree: The candidate approaches the footstool of the Master and there renounces all cowans; he promises to subdue his passions, by which means he is united to virtue and by his regularity of life demonstrates what he proposes. This is illustrated to him by the steps that he takes in approaching the altar; the symbolic meaning of which is the separation of the firmament from the earth and the water on the second day of creation.

Third Degree: Teaches us that our destiny is Death, but at the same time, in the ceremony and in the very name of Hiram, it reveals the great doctrine of another life and the immortality of the soul. The word "Hiram" in Hebrew, means "He who was or shall be raised alive or lifted up". It also symbolizes the people, rising from the death of ignorance, to the life of freedom and intelligence. Furthermore, the symbolic death of Hiram Abiff represents to us that of the Messiah; for the three blows, which were given him at the three gates of the Temple, alludes to the three points of condemnation against Jesus by the High Priests Caliphas, Herod and Pilate. If you recall it was from the last one that Jesus was led to that most violent and excruciating death. The three instruments that were used to kill Hiram are symbolic of the kiss on Jesus' cheek, the flagellation, and the crown of thorns. The brethren assembled around Hiram at the grave, is a representation of the disciples weeping over the death of Jesus on the cross. The Masters' Word, which is said to be lost since the death of Hiram Abiff, is the same that Jesus pronounced on the cross **"Eli, Eli, lama sabacthani"** (**My God, my God, why has thou forsaken me?"**) Instead of which words were substituted, M.B.N. (Mac-be-Nac) which is Arabian, signified "The son of the widow is dead." The sprig of acacia represents the cross because the cross was made of that kind of wood.

Fourth Degree: Teaches truth and consequently the existence of one God and the relations existing between man and his Heavenly Father.

Fifth Degree: Teaches us the love of God for the human race, and the magnitude of divine attributes.

Sixth Degree: Develops and fully proves the sublime and consoling doctrine of the immortality of the soul.

Seventh Degree: Teaches justice as the necessary consequence of the relations between God and man.

Eighth Degree: Teaches the necessity of order, without which society cannot exist.

Ninth Degree: Teaches us that no one has the right to take the law into his own hands.

Tenth Degree: Teaches that it does not consist with the good of society, that all should pretend to command, and that the administration of order, or the execution power, like that of justice, or the judicial power, must be confided to a few of the wisest and most experienced of the citizens.

Eleventh Degree: Teaches that the laws which are to govern a community must be elaborated, or the legislative power exercised, by the most able and honest citizens, and that to such men only it belongs, to represent the people in the legislative assemblies, there to maintain the rights and freedom of the people.

Twelfth Degree: Teaches us that by labor alone we can obtain happiness, for our fellow beings and ourselves.

Thirteenth Degree: Teaches the utility of study, as the only means of drawing nearer to our Heavenly Father, and practicing true religion, the object of which is to attain a knowledge of the perfections of God, and thereby to become more and more perfect by imitating his kindness in our relations with our brother.

Fourteenth Degree: Your receive the reward of your labors.

Fifteenth Degree: Teaches hope and faith in the new Era which draws upon mankind, when men will be emancipated from dead forms and ceremonies, and when the whole power of man's intellect will be exerted to obtain a perfect knowledge of truth, and of the laws that flow from it.

Sixteenth Degree: Teaches that every religion, of mere forms and ceremonies and external practices, must eventually crumble to pieces, for it is a dead body without soul, and that the Masonry of the Ancient and Accepted Rite, founded on the simple and pure doctrine of love, toleration and reason, must be eternal.

Seventeenth Degree: Teaches us that every good and intelligent Mason must look upon himself as a pioneer, preparing the way for greater and better men to come after him, and that he must be content to work and do his duty, whether the results of his labor are manifest and visible during his life, or not; to sow no matter who reaps.

Eighteenth Degree: Illustrates, by example, the truth of his doctrine of accumulation of intellectual wealth by inheritance, for in it are exhibited all the sublime truths, the axioms of ethics and philosophy. In this degree the new law of love is taught, and the chief pillar among the three, with which are here replaced the ancient pillars of the temple, is charity, which not only relieves the wants, but is tolerant of the errors and mistaken opinions of other men. The degree is open to men of all creeds, who believe in the fundamental doctrines of the Ancient and Accepted Rite of Masonry.

Nineteenth Degree: Teaches us that, as true apostles of the doctrine of civil and religious toleration, we must, as it were, bridge the abyss that divides us from our brethern, who adhere to the old law and ceremonial observances of the past, and win them over to us by kindness and reason.

Twentieth Degree: Teaches us the necessity of caution, in addition to energy and daring that those who tread upon and live by the propagation of false creeds, may not defeat our plans for the emancipation of human intellect.

Twenty First Degree: Teaches you to strive earnestly to learn the means necessary to vindicate the power of truth, in bringing together all God's children, whatever their religious or political opinions.

Twenty Second Degree: Teaches you that even after succeeding in that object, you would still need to be ever watchful and always on the alert, to bar the way of entrance against sectarianism.

Twenty Third Degree: Teaches that after firmly establishing the institution of the Ancient and Accepted Rite, we should profoundly study the doctrine of the master from Nazareth, and expound to our brethren of the old law its practical and sublime lessons.

Twenty Fourth Degree: Teaches us how arduous is the task of a true Mason, who endeavors to oppose sectarianism.

Twenty Fifth Degree: Teaches us to maintain the doctrine of liberty, equality and fraternity, as the only means of gathering around us the intelligent and good men of every lineage.

Twenty Sixth Degree: Teaches us how a sincere and lasting alliance may be effected between the three intellectual classes of men: The disciples of the natural law and of philosophy; those of the law of Moses, and the other ancient faith; and those who follow the doctrine of the Ancient and Accepted Rite, or the law taught by the Grand Master from Nazareth.

Twenty Seventh Degree: Teaches us that humanity is at last to become one single peaceful family, whose father and head is the eternal God, infinite in love.

Twenty Ninth Degree: Teaches us how much can be effected in a righteous cause by perseverance.

Thirtieth Degree: Teaches us to organize that army of tried and veteran Masons, that is to defend the rights of mankind against unlimited regal despotism, sacerdotal usurpation and intolerance, and the monopolies of rank, caste and privilege, and cause these usurpers to tremble, like the Babylonian King, when an awful hand wrote the word of judgment on the wall of his banquet chamber.

Thirty First: Here we learn afresh and with peculiar force the place of patient hearing, deliberate consideration and dispassionate and impartial judgment in all issues on which we must make decisions.

The candidate is then asked: What was placed in your left hand when you assumed the obligation of the 31st degree? Answer: "A pair of scales." Question: What lesson was it meant to teach you? Answer: "That in all my judgments and opinions of men, I should be guided solely by justice and equity." Question: What are the sacred words? Answer: "Justice and equity."

As mentioned earlier, members of the 32nd degree are qualified to enter the "Mystic Shrine." The Mystic Shrine is essentially a mockery of the religion of Al-Islam. Where is the Justice and equity? In the Shriners Ritual, the Chief

Rabbah states, "Who but Muhammad mingled his religion with his houri and said, "Are not these the true source of happiness?" I ask again, where is the justice and equity? Our investigation of the Shriners' Ritual reveals the highest degree of disrespect and blasphemy of the Islamic Religion.

SHRINERS ARE MASONS, NOT MUSLIMS

"In most of their secret talks, there is no good: but if one exhorts to a deed of charity, of justice, or conciliation between men (secrecy is permissible): To him who does this, seeking the good pleasure of God, we shall soon give a reward of the highest (value)."   Holy Qur'an 4:114.

It is very important that we realize that the Shriners do not advocate the religion of Al-Islam, but in fact "are required to take a solemn vow that they will redouble their courage, zeal and determination to defend and advocate the Christian religion..." Only those Masons who have received either the Knights Templar or 32nd degree of the Scottish Rite order can be initiated into the "Mystic Shrine."

The history of the Shriners' organization may be of interest to Muslims because it asserts that it was originally established in Makkah during the time of our Holy Prophet Muhammad (PBUH).

The predominant literature on the origin of the Shriners alleges that its organization (The Ancient Arabic Order of the Nobles of the Mystic Shrine) was established by Ali, the fourth Khalifah and cousin of our Holy Prophet Muhammad in the year of the Hijra 25 (A.D. 644) in the Holy City of Makkah.

According to Masonic authorities, the purpose of the order at that time was to function as an "Inquisition of Vigilance Committee, to dispense justice and execute punishment upon criminals who escaped their just deserts through the tardiness of the courts, and also to promote religious toleration among cultured men of all nations."

The Mystic Shrine "ritual" which was compiled by Noble Dr. Walter M. Fleming, 33rd degree, and Noble Williams S. Paterson, 33rd degree, who point out that the original intent of the Mystic Shrine organization was to form a cohort of rich and wealthy men, who would, "without fear or favor—upon valid accusation" of criminal activity by an individual or group—examine, judge and execute, if necessary, within the hour, in complete secrecy."

"Their ostensible object is to increase the faith and fidelity of all true believers in Allah (whose name be exalted). The secret and real purpose can only be made known to those who have encircled the Mystic Shrine according to the instructions in "The Book of the Constitution and the Regulations of the Imperial Council."

Both their explicit and esoteric objective is to misguide the "uninitiated" (non-members) and sincere believers in Allah into believing that the Shriners' goal is "to increase the faith and fidelity of all true believers in Allah (whose name be exalted)."

The esoteric and true purpose, however, can only be made known to those who have been initiated into the "Mystic Shrine" according to the guidelines set forth in the "Book of the Constitution and the Regulations of the Imperial Council." It should be emphasized here, however, that the Holy Qur'an, the last revelation from Allah, condemns double talk and deception.

It says, **"Fain would they deceive Allah and those who believe, but they only deceive themselves, and realize (it) not!"** Concerning the deceivers, Allah also says, **"When they meet those who believe, they say: 'We believe', But when they are alone with their evil ones they say: 'We are really with you, we (were) only jesting.' Allah will throw back their mockery on them, and give them rope in their trespasses; so they will wonder like blind ones (to and fro)."** (H.Q. 2:14,15).

William J. Whalen in his book, <u>Christianity and American Freemasonry</u> writes, "of course we readily admit that no Shriner seriously commits himself to the Islamic faith or considers the oath he has freely given on the Bible and the Koran (Quran) as such a profession of faith."

In the "Noble's Quiz Book" the question is asked: "Do Shriners worship Allah or accept the Mohammedan (Al-islam) religion?" Answer: "No, but belief in Deity is one of the requirements of the Order." The Shrine is called the Playground of Masonry.

Fred Van Deventer, in his book _Parade to Glory_ writes: "Shriners play Moslems (Muslims) and infidels with reverent minds and merry hearts.

The religion of Al-Islam is not a religion of foolish play and merriment. There are approximately one billion Muslims on this earth. It was this religion, as taught by Prophet Muhammad (PBUH), that enlightened the Western world with sciences and intellectual development. The Muslims invented the mathematical science of algebra and trigonometry.

Al-Islam has a track record of serious achievement and major contributions to human and societal development. As Believers, Muslims must address and combat all mockery and misrepresentation of their religion.

The Holy Quran says: **"O ye who believe! take not for friends and protectors those who take your religion for a mockery or sport. Whether among those who received the Scripture before you, or among those who reject faith, but fear ye God, if you have faith (indeed)."**

The Shriners, by their own admission, are not Muslims, but pretenders. It is reported that Prophet Muhammad (PBUH) said, **"The worse amongst the people is the double-faced one; he comes to some people with one face and to others with the other face"** (Muslim).

Imam W.Deen Muhammad said concerning the difference between true Muslims and pretenders: "Even Shriners and Masons use Quranic terminology. Though they do a great service in society, no matter how nice they are, we still condemn them using terminology of Al-Islam on that which is not Al-Islam. We have to know how to make the distinction and we have to know that the enemy of the African-American people, the racists, will do anything to keep dignity from the African-American man." (A.M. Journal, 4/20: "Know the Difference between Muslim and Devil's Dupe.")

Evidence of their Islamic pretense can be seen readily by the following quotes from the "Secret Ritual of the Ancient Arabic Order of Nobles of the Mystic Shrine": "Who so seeketh Islam earnestly, those who swerve from the truth and justice, shall merit and reap abundance of chastiesment."

The high priest says (addressing a candidate), "By the existence of Allah and the Creed of Mohammad (Muhammad): by the legendary sanctity of our Tabernacle at Mecca, we greet you, and in commemoration of the Arab's faith in purity and innocence, we accept your answers as sincere, and you will now be permitted to proceed in the rites and ceremonies of the Mystic Shrine."

The Shriner's oath includes phrases such as, "I do hereby upon this Bible and on the mysterious legend of the Koran (Quran) and its dedication to the Mohammadan faith...." It invokes the wrath of Allah upon those who break their oath.

It reads, "In willful violation whereof may I incur the fearful penalty of having my eyeballs pierced to the center with a three-edged blade, my feet flayed and I be forced to walk the hot sands upon the sterile shores of the Red Sea until the flaming sun shall strike me with livid plagues, and may Allah, the God of Arab Moslem and Mohammadan, the God of our fathers, support me to the entire fulfillment of the same, amen, amen, amen."

In addition to the blasphemies and hypocritical language that is used behind the walls of their secret temples, the Shriners openly display their deception as they parade down the city streets dressed in their red fezzes and other eastern Islamic garb.

As leader Imam W. Deen Muhammad said, "Muslims have to insist that no distorted image of our religion is given..."

"We must be strong and fearless like the companions of Prophet Muhammad (PBUH) and meet the challenge. We must accept and practice the guidance that Allah has given us in the Holy Quran and the Sunnah of Prophet Muhammad (PBUH)."

Allah says in the Quran: **"Who is better in speech than one who calls (men) to God, works righteousness, and says, 'I am of those who bow in Islam'?"** (41:33)

According to the Shriners' Recognition Test and Lecture each Shriner travels east to worship at the "Shrine of Islam." Let us observe the following dialogue: Question: "Are you a Noble of the Mystic Shrine?" Answer: "I have traveled the Arabic Path." Question: "You are a Noble then, I presume?" Answer: "I am so accepted by all men of noble birth." Question: "Have you traveled any?" Answer: "I have." Question: "From where to what place have you traveled?" Answer: "Traveled to east, over the hot burning sands of the desert." Question: "Where were you stopped at?" Answer: "At the Devil's pass." Question: "What were you requested to do?" Answer: "I was requested to contribute a few drops of urine." Question: "Why were you requested to do this?" Answer: "As a token of my renouncing the wiles and evils of the world, and be granted permission to worship at the shrine." Question: "At what shrine did you worship?" Answer: "At the shrine of Islam. Question: "Did you ride?" Answer: "Yes, I rode a camel until I was caused to dismount." Question: "Then what did you do with your camel?" Answer: "I tied him." Question: "Where did you tie him?" Answer: "I tied him to a date tree where all true and good Shriners so do".

As a Muslim, I am compelled to ask the Mason or Shriner (who perhaps is reading this right now), is it prudent and just to mingle with the precious ideas and practices of such a profound religion as Al-Islam, in a spirit of mockery and joviality?

The Holy Quran tells the Muslim and believer to, **"Leave alone those who take their religion to be mere play and amusement."** According to the Shriner's Ritual "The salutation

-208-

of distinction among the faithful is "Es Salmu Aleikum!"
Peace be with you! To which is returned the gracious wish:
"Aleikum es salaam!" With you be peace! This is a statement
of fact; however, the Quran warns us also of those who pretend
to be faithful believers but are really hypocrites. **"When
they meet those who believe they say, 'we believe,' but when
they are alone with their evil ones, they say 'we are really
with you: we (were) only jesting."** (H.Q. 2:14).

Let us observe some of the statements and teachings
of the Shriners from another point of view. Let us assume
for a moment that beneath the mockery and joviality that
there is real wisdom being taught by the Shriners, concerning
the religion of Al-Islam and the symbols that we find in
Mecca and many of the Islamic countries throughout the
world. The Shriners' Secret Ritual tells us that the secret
knowledge symbolized by the crescent always is the master
key to all wisdom. "The Greek philosopher, Plato, when
asked the source of his knowledge, referred to Pythagoras.
If we consult the writings of Pythagoras, we shall find that
he points to the Far East whence he derived his instructions.
In imitation of the humility of the wisest of mankind, we
look to the East for light, and find placed there the beautiful
emblem of newborn light, the crescent." (p.44)

The Shriners' organization seriously claims to "lead
the mind of the initiate, step by step from the sterile and
shifting sands of the desert into the halls of science, the
chambers of culture, until he stands in the presence of the
emblem of light and intelligence, in possession of the key
that will open to the intelligent inquirer every truth in nature's
wide domain". One of the Shriners's pass words is Makkah.
The Masonic writer and scholar Albert Mackey writes in
his Revised Encyclopedia of Freemasonry, the "Kaaba, the
name of the holy temple of Mecca, which is to the
Mohammedans what the temple of Solomon was to the Jews.
It is certainly older, as Gibbon admits, than the Christian
era, and is supposed by the tradition of the Arabians, to
have been erected in the nineteenth century before Christ,
by Abaraham, who was assisted by his son Ishmael. It derives
its name of Kaaba from its cubical farm, it being fifteen
feet long, wide and high." (Vol 2, p.513). The Masonic Quiz
Book states: "Mecca, a City in Arabia, 60 m. from the Red

Sea and birthplace of Mohammead" (p.269). According to the Shriners symbolic teachings, the word Makkah is symbolized by the word Rebecca which is a play on the Semitic term Bekkah, which means crying. Imam Warith Deen Muhammad writes, "And Makkah was originally called Bekkah. It means, 'She was crying.' Crying for what? Because her sciences had been polluted. Her sciences had been stolen, misused, and polluted. So she was crying. But when Allah brought Prophet Muhammad (PBUH) there, she stopped crying and she became Makkah. Praise be to Allah.

"In Makkah we find a great symbol, the Kaabah, a cube. All its sides are square: it has a square as a base, it has a square on all its walls, and it has a square at its top. Its angles are pretty well equal, they are supposed to be symbolic of balance, material balance. The Kaaba, a square, is in a circle. The Haji makes seven circles around the Kaaba." Imam Muhammad continues, "There is a square sitting in a circle, meaning your material conscience should be surrounded and it should be protected by taqwah (God consciousness)....We make seven circles around the Kaabah, symbolic of ethics. Allah wants us to evolve ethics on the basis of what is materially needed in man's life..."

In another play on words, Masonic catechism symbolizes the Biblical figure Tubalcain, by two balls and a cain. The two balls represent circles or spiritual consciousness. If we observe the heavenly bodies, they look round like a ball. The Bible says Jesus took some of his disciples on top of a mountain and showed them two round lights in the heavens. The cain represents the staff of Moses which, according to the Masonic writer Steinmetz, is symbolic of knowledge and wisdom. He writes, "In the courts of Pharaoh, Moses instructed Aaron to cast down his rod and it changed into a serpent, the symbol of wisdom....We are to understand that thenceforth he had wisdom upon which to learn." (The Royal Arch Its Hidden Meaning, p. 107). We also learn that Tubalcain represents industry. The Bible says, Tubalcain was an instructor of every artifice in brass and iron; he was a descendent of Cain who killed his brother Abel or human ability.

THE SHRINERS' EMBLEM

Let us look briefly at the Shriners' Emblem. The ritual says the Jewel of the Shriners' Order is a cresent formed of any substance, but the most valued materials are the claws of the Bengal tiger. United at their bases is a gold setting which includes their tips and bears on one side of the center the head of a sphinx and on the other a pyramid, urn and star with the arabic motto "Kuwat wa Ghadab" (Strength and Fury). The Shriners wear the Cresent turned downward with a sword over it, according to their teaching. "For esoteric reasons we hang the horns pointing downward representing the setting moon of the old faith at the moment of the rising sun of the new faith in the brotherhood of all mankind--the essential unity of humanity as of one blood, the children of one fatherhood."

A further analysis of the emblem reveals that the sword is placed over the Sphinx, the pyramid and the cresent because it represents the Sacred Word (S-Word) of truth that rules over the four elements that are symbolized in both the sphinx and the pyramid.

The Fez: Perhaps the reader has noticed that the Shriners wear the fez like some Muslims do. According to Masonic teaching the fez is a mark of learning and scholarship. It is said that when the pilgrimage to Makkah was interrupted by the Crusades, about A.D. 980, the Muslims west of the Nile journeyed to Fas (or fez) in Morocco, as to a holy city. "Among the flourishing manufactuers of the city was a head covering called tashboosh, now known as a fez which was dyed scarlet for students in a great school in that city. In that way it became a mark of learning..."

THIRTY-THIRD DEGREE

Thirty Third Degree: The last and final degree of Ancient and Accepted Scottish Rite Freemasonry is called "Sovereign Grand Inspector General." This degree is generally defined as the administrative degree of the order. The meetings are called a Supreme Council. The jewel is a black double headed eagle with golden beaks and claws, holding in the latter a gold sword, and crowned with the golden crown of Prussia. A red tuitonic cross is affixed to the left side of the breast. The lodge is hung with purple curtains, on which are painted skeletons, death heads, cross, bones, etc. There are nine officers in this degree. The Master of the lodge is called the "Most Puissant Sovereign Grand Commander." During the opening ceremonies the Master of the Lodge asks the Puissant Lieutenant Grand Commander: "From whence came you?" Answer: "From the cradle, passing through life towards our common lot—the grave."

After the lodge is declared opened the Master of the lodge orders the Gtrand Marshal to prepare the candidate (if there is one) for initiation by divesting him of his shoes and hat, clothe him in a black robe, give him a lighted candle in his right hand, tie a black rope around his neck, and lead him (like a helpless animal) to the door of the council chamber. It is said to the candidate, once he enters the council chamber and is received by the image of a skeleton, "Your head is uncovered, your feet bare to remind you that you must ever be prepared to assist brethren in need, and free them from the yoke of oppression, which is symbolized by the black cabletow around your neck." We also learn in this degree that the object of all the degrees in Masonry is light, wisdom, tolerance, freedom and courage. It is also revealed in this degree that all the ceremonies of Masonry are but "faithful" representations of the realistic life. Those who are initiated into the 33rd degree are reminded that Masonry "recognizes and adopts none of the religions of the world."

It is important to note here that this degree attempts to pull together the teachings of the former degrees. It gives a more profound explanation of Masonic ceremonies. The Illustrious Grand Minister of State explains in a lecture to the candidate and the general body 33rd degree members, that the object is not to rebuild the material temple of Solomon, but a moral temple, wherein truth and love shall dwell. Concerning the Hiramic Legend, he says, "We have not to avenge the murder of Hiram Abiff, for he represents that eternal wisdom, which ignorance and lust of power and falsehood had concealed from us, but we must go on, in search of those laws by which the moral world is regulated. We have not persecuted the unfortunate nation of Judah, for having sentenced to death our beloved Sovereign Jesus of Nazareth, the Apostel of the duties and rights of man, but we must crush forever superstition, fanaticism and intolerance. They, and not the children of Israel were guilty.

"To no man has God given authority to replace and represent Him on earth, and all those who pretend to be His ministers and representatives must not be believed. Our ignorance and selfishness alone give these usurpers the power, which they wield for the gratification of their emperors' schemes. Our Order is instituted to stop such encroachment and to prevent the renewal of the tragedy which ended in the murder of those Kinght Templars, whose virtues and moral powers caused such terror to the political and religious usurpers of that age." He further points out that Freemasonry abhors the doctrine which teaches the murder of kings and priests "but as long as the weakness of mankind renders their usurpation unavoidable, we must prevent their exercising their power to oppress mankind and endeavor by degrees to enlighten our brother men."

After the lecture the candidate is taught the pass-words, signs and motto of this degree:

PASSWORD - De Molay, Hiram Abiff, "Frederick", of Prussia.

SIGN OF ORDER: Place the left hand over the heart.

SIGN OF ENTRANCE: Cross the arms on the breast and bow the head.

MOTTO OF THE ORDER: "D us Meumgue Jus" (My God and my Right)

CONCLUSION

There is much more that can be said about Freemasonry, but time and space will not allow us to expound any further at this point. I hope and pray to Allah that the reader was able to derive some knowledge from our research. Our aim was not to attack or offend any individual, only to share the information that we were blessed to receive. Knowledge is preserved and purified by its constant flow from one person to another. It is like the flowing water of a mighty stream. Once the Freemasons, and other secret societies come to realize this, the better off they will be. Those who conceal and hide the knowledge that God has freely given for the benefit of humanity are no less than thieves and robbers. According to my research much of the precious knowledge of the ancient wise people of Africa is lost because it was stolen and locked up in secret vaults. If the seeds of knowledge is not watered and allowed to blossom forth under the light of openness, it becomes obsolete and dies in the dry soil of darkness and secrecy.

> 'What God out of His mercy
> Doth bestow on mankind
> There is none can withhold:
> What He doth withhold,
> There is none can grant,
> Apart from Him:
> And He is the Exalted
> in power, Full of Wisdom.
>
> **Holy Qur'an 35:2**